INTO

HIS

GLORIOUS

LIGHT

RACHAEL HAVERPORTH

"But you are a chosen people, a royal priesthood, a holy nation,
a people for God's own possession, to proclaim the virtues of Him who
called you out of darkness into His marvelous light"
1 Peter 2:9

TRILOGY
A WHOLLY OWNED SUBSIDIARY OF **TBN**
PROFESSIONAL PUBLISHING MEETS POWERFUL PROMOTION

Trilogy Christian Publishers

A Wholly Owned Subsidiary of Trinity Broadcasting Network

2442 Michelle Drive

Tustin, CA 92780

For information, address Trilogy Christian Publishing

Rights Department, 2442 Michelle Drive, Tustin, Ca 92780.

For information about special discounts for bulk purchases, please contact Trilogy Christian Publishing.

10 9 8 7 6 5 4 3 2 1

Library of Congress Cataloging-in-Publication Data is available.

ISBN 979-8-89333-831-7

ISBN 979-8-89333-832-4 (ebook)

TABLE OF CONTENTS

DEDICATION

I dedicate this book to all the broken people who are in the process of healing. The ones who are too afraid to talk about their pain. To the people who are about to go through their own healing journey. I want to encourage you to keep pushing through. I know it is hard, but there is such a beautiful story for you waiting on the other side. There is freedom like you have never known. There is a loving Father who wants to shower you with love. Be honest with Him. God is good, loving, and safe. He did not start you on this journey without giving you the tools you need to make it through. I encourage you to meet the God you have always wanted to know.

Special thanks go to the people who helped me find wisdom, love, truth, and victory. I know you prayed for me. I know you went outside of your comfort zone to help me. I love the unity that happened and how God used it. Thank you, Brittany Grace, Tyler Grace, Sierra Grace, Rebekah Weaver, Rachel Banister, Jacob Merz, Sheila Perry, and Ben House. Without you by my side, I would not have made it.

Thank you, Carol Basile, for being an advisor and making this book come alive in a beautiful way.

Most of all, thank you, Trinity, for grabbing my hand and walking me through the most painful time of my life. You were always loving, kind, truthful, and patient. I will never forget this unforgettable journey you have agreed to be on with me.

Rachael Haverporth

INTRODUCTION

I started writing this book in November of 2021. I had no idea that this would be the book God was asking me to write. I only knew that I was struggling. I wanted to know who God is. I was asking myself three main questions:

God, are You good?

God, are You safe?

God, do You love me?

I was asking God to reveal His character to me. I had no idea that I had a false belief that God would hurt me. At a point in this journey, I asked God if He was an abuser. All I wanted when I started on this journey was to get married. I had no idea that it would take more than three years for everything to be settled, and I would have to walk through my childhood trauma, redefine my relationships, and figure out who God really is and who I really am.

There is no narrative in this story. It is a compilation of my blogs and poems. This is what I felt in each stage of my healing. It has happened in real time; it is my real emotions and shows my incremental growth. These blogs and poems are the chronicles of a painful but necessary healing journey. On the journey, I had godly friends, Christian movies and books, and, most importantly, the Trinity walking with me. I did not have a professional counselor or educated person with a degree to guide me. It was all God and me and our one-on-one conversations.

Truthfully, most of the time, I was yelling, screaming, and

wanting to give up. I am not going to lie: there were many times I almost took my own life. I was fed up, tired, and confused. I felt hopeless, and I saw no way out. Through it all, a loving God met me while I indulged in my raging temper. He did not ask me to be perfect. He wanted honesty and vulnerability. It was messy, it was difficult, and it could have cost me my life. Was it worth it in the end? Yes, because you cannot cover up "broken." You cannot cover up the pain. The only way to healing is through Jesus Christ. My desire is that through my pain and vulnerability, you also will find healing or at least find the beginning of the healing path. I hope God speaks to someone through my story. If it helps someone survive the pain of molestation, suicidal thoughts, or restoration of a relationship with Christ, I am grateful God has used my testimony for good.

We all want to be loved. We all want to be free and know who we are. Here is my unique, beautifully complicated story of how God transformed me to help me see who He is and who He says I am. He is a God who is safe, loves me, and is so good. He is a God who always shows up and reveals His character. He is more than enough, and He is the Healer. Here is my beautiful fairy tale with a loving God.

Note: I wrote the prologue on the following pages a year before I wrote the poems. I had no idea that it would be a prophecy to everything that was going to happen. I did not re-read it until seven months later. It made me cry to see how God did not hide what He was about to do. He revealed this journey to me in January 2021, a year prior to the drafting of this book.

PROLOGUE

I am writing this story because God asked me to write His story, and I want to be faithful to Him. This story is a lifetime story. It is a story of trauma, pain, love, lies and truth. This story is not for the weak of heart. It is not a story to make you feel good and smile. It is not a typical love story. As I write this story, I don't even know what the ending will be. God is still writing my love story. I believe the main reason I am writing a book is to document my healing. Writing this is making me step out in extreme faith, hope, and love. God also knows I am the least likely to write since my whole life, I was told I did not have the talent to do so.

I do not know how this story will end, but I do know the Author of this story. I know how much He has healed me and changed me and answered some big prayers that I have been praying. I know that during this time, He has changed me into the woman He always intended me to be. Right now, I am hurting. Right now, I have big questions. This story is about Love. What is it really? How can one obtain a 1 Corinthians 13 love here on earth? It is about asking God tough questions and not being afraid of His answers. It is about living past my emotions and standing on the one true Rock, who is God.

I started 2020 off with a desire to work on my ability to hope, have faith, and love. I had just surrendered some things to God and had no idea where that journey would take me. God has made me big promises, and I was too afraid to believe Him. I fought, and I questioned, but I stepped out in faith. First, I needed to surrender my biggest heart's desire. Now, I could see it coming true, but I was also afraid to have hope. I was afraid to be happy. I was afraid of God failing me. Yes, I said it. Sorry, but it is true. I have always had a heart for God, but because of some very deep wounds, I had issues with trust, love, faith, and hope. It has been a source of pain for me for thirty years. I have struggled. I have not been happy.

I always wanted to know the heart of God. I always wanted to pursue Him. However, something was missing. I was tormented with these thoughts for years. In times that should have been my happiest, that should have been full of joy, hope, and answered prayers, I was still miserable. I was still tormented. Why? The truth is I was never willing to go through my pain with God. I was never willing to let Him search my heart and know me. I was too ashamed to let Him see how messed up I really was. Then how could I ever be the Proverbs 31 wife or mother I was so desperately praying to be?

When I started to have hope, faith, and love, the promises seemed to be pulled from me. I began a journey with God that created the most healing I have ever had. I finally was willing to start being truthful with Him. I was so desperate for the excitement of the promises that were taken from me that I did what I knew how to do best: I legalistically went after His heart, but in pursuit of my promises, He tore my legalism from me and showed me how to stand in faith.

Finally, I have real joy and hope. Now I understand unconditional love. I would have never asked for God to answer my prayers or make good on His promises in this way. Now, I can see that this is God's way of answering my biggest prayers. God did it in His own unique way. The only way that would work for me. God knows me, and He loves me, so He created the most beautiful love story.

I have found the only way to have a transformed and godly heart is to be willing to walk through your pain with God. I have stepped through each door of pain with God by my side. By doing this, I found out who He really is and who I really am. I am no longer hiding. I am being honest. It is not pretty, and it is not conventional. It has not been easy, and I have fought hard. I still have days when I question if I am crazy or just have crazy faith. I still wonder why God loves me when I am so difficult. I do not understand why things happen the way they do. I do not understand why something that feels so wrong can still be in God's perfect timing or God's perfect will or why something that hurts so bad can be God's goodness. I guess I must accept that I do not always get to know the why, just the Who. God is good. God is love. God is hope, and God has a good future for me. If I walk with Him, if I stay in His timing and His will, then He will change my life.

What you are about to read is God's unique and beautiful love story. I do not have an ending because I am still waiting for it to happen. I would not have guessed it would go this way. The only way this story makes sense is through God. It is His testimony. Only God can take two broken people with broken pasts who have been praying for years and put them together in one big answer to prayer. I have been praying for God to work it all out, and now I realize that I am the miracle He has provided. The miracle is what He has done in me and the freedom I have found in my most painful season. It is also the truth He has revealed in me and how He has saved me from my tormented past.

I get to be the main character in this story, and God has an amazing love story for me, which is a double blessing. However, the fairy tale must start first with Him and me. I believe in faith and prayer, and from what God has told me, the second fairy tale happens after I and the man God promised me walk through our own pain to come face to face with God and believe He is our friend, our Father, and our Bridegroom.

For me, this is the greatest and most unique love story. For ten years, I have prayed for this, but God had to dramatically change my heart before He began revealing the answer. I had to learn to let Him create the story by surrendering to His plan no matter how much I did not understand it. We will all find out together what the answer is because the story continues and is being slowly unveiled until we reach the end of it.

THE GREATEST LOVE STORY

God has always told me that He had the most amazing love story for me, which is interesting because if you know me, you know I hate romances. I was always into sports, action, and comedies. Even as a kid, I wasn't much into Disney fairy tales. They were not my style. One day, when I was watching *Beauty and the Beast*, God showed me that He had a story for me like a fairy tale. Truthfully, I believe that God does have an actual love story for me, but it is on pause because I first had to learn how to know, love, and trust the Author of the love story. I needed to experience the greatest love story of all time: God's love story for me.

Once upon a time, there was a princess. This princess was loved by everyone around her, and they considered her beautiful. She laughed without fear of the future. She ran in her father's garden and enjoyed life. She was carefree. Her father gave her anything she wanted. She was the happiest, most joyful little princess you could ever meet. She had a large inheritance, and the entire world valued and honored her. When she was very young, she ran into someone she thought was her friend, but this was not a friend. This person abused her and took away her innocence. It was a dark day indeed. The princess no longer felt safe to run in her father's garden. She felt shame and no longer felt beautiful. She felt confused and dirty. However, she pretended to be beautiful even though she didn't feel like it. She decided that no one would know how much shame she really felt. Then, one day, the princess forgot the whole incident. She continued living as if nothing had happened. She was as happy as she could be, except for one small thing: she felt the need to protect herself. She no longer felt like her father could do it. After all, the princess reasoned, he didn't stop what happened before. The princess was no longer a young girl. She was now a woman. She wanted to do what was right and please her father, but she wanted to have fun, too. So, after years of drinking, partying, and too many boys, she forgot who she was. She only went to her father in times of great need but decided only she could protect herself.

She no longer wanted to be a princess but would rather work and be independent. She wanted to do what she wanted. Her father let her leave because he loved her and would not interfere with her free will. She still loved her father and trusted him with some things, but she was going to do what she was going to do. With her wounds, her habits, and denial, she soon lived a fake but highly successful life. She looked good on the outside but could not be happy on the inside. She started hating herself, and she could not understand why her father would treat her with respect. She felt like she was dirty, a failure, a drunk, a cutter, and suicidal. Who would love a princess who chose to be a slave? Even though she knew her father loved her and that she was choosing to be a slave, she still chose to live this way, no longer dressing in beautiful clothes and enjoying the inheritance of her father's beautiful household or the gardens. She would return for quick visits, but when life got hard, she returned to her life as a slave.

This story sounds far-fetched or even child-like. But this is my story. My whole life, I have tried to protect myself. I was angry, and I tried to control everything. God gave me a perfect gift and the promise of a love story, but I couldn't accept it. God spoke clearly to me. He said, *"Rachael, it is time for you to find out who really loves you, who is the Author of this love story, the One who created your perfect fairy tale…Me!"* Since then, I have lost, and I have won. I surrendered, then took it back. I have hated so many parts of me, then found so many parts of me that I love. For the first time, I have had to heal without any of my protection mechanisms, my control, or my addictive devices. I have had to heal, love, and live life with my perfect Bridegroom. God! There is no other story than the love story of a savior who has put up with me, my addictions, my self-sabotage, my pain, my anger, my hate, and my out-of-control rage. But God never leaves. I do not have to hide or be perfect for Him. He loves me no matter what. He is never annoyed by me or thinks less of me. He loves me in my imperfections and makes me perfect in Him. He loves me, and then He proves it.

I had to lose something that I found to be special to realize that I had not let God have my whole heart. My healing has come in increments, but I needed my deepest wounds to be revealed before they could be healed. For the first time in my life, I decided to go through this painful season without relying on any of my addictions (i.e., crutches). I have not had a drop of alcohol, weed, pills, self-abuse, control, or sabotage to fall back on. I only have my Savior, my Bridegroom, to keep me. For the first time in my life, I've realized that God is enough for me. I have put Him on the throne of my life. I have learned not to control Him but to let Him lead me. I have let Him expose deep lies that I have believed for so long. He told me the biggest lie that caused me to run away my entire life is that I have to protect myself. Opening doors before His timing does not require faith. So, I choose not to open any doors. I choose to stay in His perfect timing. I choose to let Him lead me where He wants me. I choose to have faith in Him. During this painful time, I went back and read my prayer journal. I realized God is just answering all my prayers. It may not look like what I thought it would. However, it is perfect. I have been praying for nine years. This has been my heart's desire to share my life with a godly man and have a godly legacy. Having it put on hold hurt me more than I could imagine, but finding God as my Bridegroom, finding my childlike faith in Him, and having His heart (like I prayed for) is my actual heart's desire.

My heart is whole because I know God loves me and calls me His princess. I do not have to be ashamed. He wants the best for me and wants to fight my battles. I know that He has the best love story of all time for me, which is worth everything to me. I have been a slave for too long, and that was never God's intention. He always wanted me to be His princess and experience His greatest love story. For the first time in my life, I want to watch Him just do what He is going to do. I want to watch Him love His daughter and make the love story that He always had for me unfold. I know

He can protect me and wants the best for me. I want to completely surrender even if I don't get the prince in the end because I get the Father no matter what. What more could I ever want? I have freedom like I have never had before. I have peace that surpasses all understanding. I get to walk with Him through my pain into the most beautiful places. *Freedom*. I get to hear my God call me His princess and lavish me with love. I don't need anything more. This princess is finally home and no longer a slave. She is experiencing love and dancing in her Father's presence. No one can steal her innocence anymore. She is with her Father, and she is loved.

Do not let the world steal your fairy tale. God also wants you to be free and no longer a slave. Please don't wait for heartache to learn this. Please run to Him today and let Him heal you and give you your freedom. He knows your pain and your shame. He still loves you. He calls you His own. You are His princess or prince. *Go home to your Father; you are not a slave.*

A DIFFERENT WAY TO SEE THE GREATEST LOVE STORY EVER

I have had a lot of healing since writing the earlier blog. At that time, I told the story out of a heart that was full of pain. I wrote the best love story I could, considering I did not understand real love. So, let's start again. This time, I will skip the fairy tale and tell it straight forward. I am in a very vulnerable place in my life, but I think it is important to share this story from all facets of my healing journey. I believe it:

1. helps me heal,

2. allows me to be vulnerable and transparent, and;

3. gives all the glory to God when you see the results, breakthroughs, and answered prayers.

So, here we go…

Last week, God asked me to fast from food and spend a day with Him. It resulted in an amazing day full of breakthroughs and freedom. The next day, I woke up crying. I cried at church. I cried in the car. I cried, then I cried some more. I was on the floor begging God to search my heart and show me why I continue to have days of freedom and then days like today. I have never been so willing and open for Him to have my whole heart and transform me. I am willing to die to myself and live in the spirit. I want to be new. I want to be who God wants me to be. What is holding me back?! Big prayers bring big results, and when you ask the flesh to die so the spirit can live, it results in a battle. So today, with a soft voice, I told my flesh: *It's okay, you can rest. You did the best job you could, but now it's time for the spirit to take over. It's time to let the Holy Spirit lead.* Then the craziest thing happened—I felt peace. I had been praying, fasting, and worshiping all day, and then discovered that all I had to do was rest and say those words. I think sometimes we try too hard. God wants my freedom more than I do. He wants to love me more than I want to be loved. I don't have to beg. I don't have to do anything but just let Him. We also give the enemy too much credit. It wasn't him I was fighting today; it was me and my own flesh, but I am getting ahead of my-self. Let's go back to how God even got me here.

Shortly after writing my last blog, I got stuck. I did not know how to deal with the trauma I had gone through when I was five. So, I went to my trusted prayer partners and friends who have experience with God and healing. While they ministered to me, I became angry and felt numb. I tried to heal through my own willpower. After hearing a little girl's voice screaming at me and saying that it was no big deal, I thought to myself that maybe the voice was right. However, I chose to ignore the voice and what it was saying. I told God I would let Him pursue my whole heart. Then I heard Him say that I needed to let Him in. I was probably angry for the first forty-five minutes. My friends and I asked God what to do. Then God showed me that I did not trust Him with my pain, I did not want to have emotions, and I did not trust Him. He also showed me that the trauma *was* a big deal because it was hiding my choices from me.

Trauma had been hiding my choices for my entire life. I repent-ed for not trusting God, and He started restoring what was lost and broken. I walked in a lot of freedom until the day before Thanksgiving of that year. Although I know I was hearing God loud and clear, I felt like I was trying to control His instructions and open a door out of God's timing. That is when I consulted with my prayer partners. We all agreed what I thought God was telling me to do was not a good idea. This brought up another issue for me. What if I had not been hearing from God for the last six months? What if I were crazy? Who am I if I don't hear from God and I don't get my promise? What is left of me? I struggled with these questions for a few days, and it was feeding my confusion instead of helping me see clearly what is God and what is not. *(Continue reading to find out what God revealed to me.)*

After a few days, I received *more* freedom when I realized I had emotional addictions. I had already addressed and conquered my physical addictions, but now I have discovered that I also have emotional ones. God revealed that my need to know the reasoning of things is an emotional addiction for me. This addiction has ruined my relationships for years, but God showed me that I cannot be rejected, abandoned, or not loved because He loves me. Man cannot take that away from me. The biggest thing I have learned is I have a choice. I can *choose* to let my emotions control me, and I can *choose* to let people hurt me, *or* I can *choose* to believe what God says about me. It might seem silly to you, but I never knew I had this choice. I was a slave to my emotions and never knew it. Essentially, I was a slave to other people and their decisions. What a sad and scary life to live. I can't control other people, but I let them control me. What hope would I have if I continued living this way? I also realized that other people are allowed to make choices that I may not agree with, but that does not mean they are wrong. Their choices do not have to affect me. They are allowed their choices, and I am allowed to respect that without needing to control their choices. I realized that their choices do not control me, and my choices do not control them. There is no reason to get angry or try to control their free will. I also realized I can take every thought captive. I can choose how I think, what I say, and how I act. I am not a victim; I am a conqueror. I get to die to my old self and make my highest choice.

As I struggled with all this, God taught me two new and very important things. He asked me, *"Do you love Me or yourself like I command in 1 Corinthians 13:4–8?"* Love is patient; love is kind... You know the scripture. I am never afraid to ask God a question or answer God's tough questions because they bring freedom. However, after He asked me this question, I realized that I don't love God or myself like 1 Corinthians 13. If I did, every time something bad happens I would not withdraw my love from God, the people in the situation, or myself. I had to hear that answer come from my mouth. "No, God, I don't truly love You, myself, or anyone with that kind of love." That's a tough pill to swallow. So, I surrendered to Him. I said, "God, I love You, and You love me."

I repeated 1 Corinthians 13 over and over until I believed it. Then I said, "I will love myself and others." I repeated 1 Corinthians 13 until I believed it. The biggest breakthrough yet was learning how to love, learning how to love without fear, learning how to love without strings attached, learning how to love without expectations, and learning how to love without running away because I may get hurt. I want God to be the Author of my love story—of all my stories. I realized that there is no love story if you don't know how to love. In these circumstances, I learned what it meant when God said He loves me. If He loves me, He can't want me to be harmed. He can't want me to suffer. So today, I choose to love God back. I choose to give up all my addictions. I choose to trust Him and not open my own doors. I choose to change my thinking patterns, my emotions, and my words. I choose God over my circumstances. I choose to give God my pain and not let my pain control me. I choose to walk through this with God. Accepting His love has given me joy, peace, and hope. I finally understand what it means to be free. I finally understand what it means to not be a slave. I say it all the time, but finally, I know what it means to know the Author of the greatest love story and to be *a daughter of a King*.

So, "How is this a love story?" you might ask. I was trapped for twenty-nine years. I did not know I could make choices since my choices were hidden from me. I acted out of a five-year-old's protective mechanisms, and my relationships all failed. I never understood why or why I was a victim. When God came after my heart, I fought Him. I yelled at Him. I made Him the bad guy while proclaiming that He was good, that I loved Him, and that I trusted Him. However, I really did not believe what I was saying. I blamed Him for everything. I opened my own doors and walked out of His will. I told Him "No" all the time. The more I acted out, the harder He pursued me. He did it in a loving way and the only way that would work for me. In a situation when I would usually give up, be angry, and walk away, He decided to change my heart. He answered all my prayers. He gave me a new heart—one like His that allows me to love when I don't think it's fair and to trust even when it is difficult. I can see He is good even when the promise has not yet manifested. He showed me how to pursue Him with a healed heart, to surrender my emotional addictions, my control, my defenses, and my need to make my own way. He showed me how to love like He loves. For the first time, I have peace because I know that if God loves me, He won't retract His promises. His will is perfect, and He wants me to be in His perfect will. When

I love Him, I stay in that perfect will. This is the first time I have ever really understood the truth of this. It makes me giddy and gives me that child-like faith I have been praying for. I know He is my Father, and I can blindly trust Him and live in the moment.

I confess that I have never enjoyed my life. People always said how amazing my life looked but I could never live in the moment and enjoy it. I was always thinking about tomorrow. However, God has now shown me to just stay in the moment. I have more joy right now in the middle of tough circumstances and an unknown future than I did when I was on vacation in Hawaii. Why? Because I am just staying in the moment with God and enjoying His presence. I am learning how to surrender to Him and just wait on Him to do His thing. I am laughing and crying with joy because I am so excited to see what He is going to do and how He is going to do it. In the end, I can say, "Look, only God could do this."

I have learned to choose how I want to act, think, and speak. I am beginning to bring them into alignment with His Word. I have learned to dance, sing, and worship Him even when my world seems to be falling apart. I have learned that it does not matter if I heard Him wrong. At least I trust Him enough to ask. At least I have enough faith to trust God in all situations. Plus, I know I hear from Him. I have learned that I can rest and do nothing. He will fight my battle for me. He will do it in His perfect timing and in His perfect way. It will be good. I can trust Him. I don't have to know the answers but just follow the One who has them, step by step, day by day. I have a new identity and a new name: it is *Beloved Daughter of a King*.

I am no longer a slave. I am no longer a victim. I am highly favored, I am redeemed, I am restored. I am loved. I am healed. I am a conqueror. I have an inheritance. I am walking in victory. I am God's chosen. I am worthy. I am enough. I have a future and a hope. So, tell me, do you know a greater love story than this?

And She Lived Happily Ever After

THE JOURNEY TO UNDERSTANDING GOD'S LOVE

You can call me Frodo Baggins because, boy, I have been on an adventure for the last six weeks. I am a long way away from the Shire. What I thought was a comfortable home was really my prison cell. Although this journey has been difficult, and I have met some trolls, orcs, and bad wizards on the way, I have come out in victory. In my adventure of learning who I really am in Christ and who the Author of my great love story is, I have experienced great pain but also great freedom. Just like in Lord of the Rings, I needed to throw my ring (control, emotional bondage, and bad thought patterns) into the fire of Mordor (God's refining fire). Here is my continuing journey to understanding God's love.

I have recently come to realize my story has been a progression of how I see and accept God in my life. I started on this leg of the journey when I rededicated my life through baptism.

I had just gotten out of a four-year toxic relationship with my live-in boyfriend (please don't judge). I had just failed my physical therapy boards. I had also lost all my friends and felt very alone. I was a secret alcoholic (or so I thought), suicidal, a negative thinker, and an emotional wreck. *(My mom told me recently she was very afraid that I was going to try to commit suicide again during this time of my life.)* I was pretty much at rock bottom. Then, a strange thing happened. I realized that my life was out of control, and I decided to surrender my life to God and start over. That's when I got baptized. As I sat on the stairs before getting baptized, I cried my eyes out as I told God He could have my life. I somehow knew that I would look back at my life in a year and be amazed at what He had done with my life. That was the beginning of my annual life reviews. At the beginning of the year, I reflect on what God has done in my life. I am always astounded.

At the time of my baptism, God became my close friend. I wanted to spend time with Him. I liked talking to Him. I would listen to His opinions, and I sometimes took them into consideration. I decided to control my drinking, but I wasn't going to stop drinking. I stopped sleeping around, but I didn't stop chasing men who held no future for me. I prayed but didn't necessarily listen. I listened to God's advice, but ultimately, it did not change my decision. I respected Him if He did not get in my way, but I still did what I wanted. I called Him my bestie and said I wanted to make Him happy, but at the end of the day, I still chose me and my will. To my surprise, God still loved me. He still talked to me. He still gave me choices and came after my heart. He respected my will and continued to be my close friend while He waited for me to let Him in a little more.

I chose to let God be my father figure a few years ago when I stopped drinking. I had gotten to the point in my walk with God that I wanted to obey Him. I wanted to surrender my physical addictions to Him. I chose to listen to Him and move forward with Him every day. However, like with my real father, I questioned Him all the time. I still fought Him and would usually do the exact opposite of what He asked. Later, I would realize He was right, apologize, and then do the right thing. As my walk continued to grow, I could see that when I obeyed God, I had victory. I stopped questioning Him as much. I spent more time with Him, and I listened to Him to a greater extent. I really valued God as my Father. I respected His opinion, and I asked for it more often. However, I still chose to take the lead in my life. I argued with Him. I continually told Him, "No."

I said I loved Him with my whole heart, but I repeatedly questioned Him. I was trying to figure out His character and thought, *Well, sometimes fathers are wrong.* Sometimes, I followed His example. Sometimes, I listened. Mostly, I was wildly in love with Him. However, I continued to act like a wild teenager and rebelled against Him. I did what I wanted when I was angry with Him. I knew for years I was missing something in my walk with God. It bothered me for a long time. I had all these areas I hid from God. I mean, do you really want to talk about your impure thoughts, your anger, or your lust with your father!? I felt helpless in my thought life and my emotions for years, which affected my walk with God. But God met me where I was and loved me no matter what. I grew in my walk with God. Then, one day, truth hit my lies, and I knew that my walk with God had to change.

For months, I had been praying big prayers. "Be careful what you ask for." Isn't that what they say? When you spend time in the prayer closet, God starts to do things in your life. When you ask God to be your Bridegroom and to move you onwards in your life, He presents you with the opportunity to do just that. God wanted my full freedom. He wanted my victory; He wanted my whole heart, which He cannot have if I only see Him as my Father. He wants to be my Bridegroom. I had been praying for that for years, not knowing what it meant. I was about to find out what it meant. As I surrendered to Him completely, as I put my faith in Him, I learned to love Him in a 1 Corinthians way. So naturally the next step was to invite Him into my heart to be my Bridegroom. I looked up the vows for a real wedding. I put our names in the vows. I wrote the Ten Commandments down and swore to follow them. Then, I wrote my own personal vows to God.

I had such freedom. I was like a whole new person until emotional overload happened. It was like a punch to the stomach. I tried to stay strong, but my five-year-old showed up again. She was trying to protect me. I acted out. I started to question the character of God again. *Are You worthy to be my leader? Are You good? Do You have my best interest in mind? Will You hurt me?* This may sound silly, but I bet if you think about it, you may find you also question God in these areas. Do you still argue with God? Do you say no to Him? If the answer is yes to any of these questions, then you, too, question His character.

In His infinite love, God answered these questions for me. He was not angry. God is not offended by your tough questions. I was stuck in my emotions and the five-year-old state of mind. I wrestled with self-will and free will. Which one would I give to God? I was sick to my stomach at this point. I had a migraine, and I had been crying for the better part of the day. I felt that I had gone back to ground zero, and I was disgusted with myself. I kept asking myself, "Why would God make a promise to me and not keep it? Why would He then make it look like He was going to fulfill the promise and then cancel it? Why would He repeatedly tell me it was going to be great, but it was turning out horrible? Why would God get my hopes up when I asked Him not to? Why would He make it look like a miracle was about to happen and then call it off? Why would I want a Bridegroom like that?"

I fought, and I fought, and I fought until I was too exhausted. I had no more fight left in me. I realized I had not come this far to go back. This was the next step, and I needed to take it. So, I told the five-year-old that she no longer needed to protect me. She could rest. I no longer needed to fight or question God. I realized that I was having an emotional addiction episode with God and trying to control Him. That does not work and is not healthy. For now, I tucked His promise into my heart, and I know He will answer it. I do not need to know how or when. I just need to know my Bridegroom is perfect and He will do what He says in His perfect time. I have chosen to trust Him, to get to know His true character, to learn to love Him unconditionally, and to be His bride. I am finally free.

I asked God some questions the other day. He sent me to a verse that revealed to me that I was asking the wrong question. I didn't know what that meant at the time, but I do now. I apologize for focusing on the wrong thing in these last three blogs. In asking the wrong questions, I have concentrated on the wrong story. When talking about your love story, the question to ask is not "Who am I?" but "Who is the God living in me?" The answer is the Bridegroom. He is all that matters. My life is no longer my own. It is His. He is love and truth. He is the Love Story. My job as His bride is to say "yes and amen" and to love like He loves. So please let me introduce you to the only thing that matters. The Author of my love story and yours as well. The One I should have been focusing on the whole time, Christ.

God is love. God is good. God is the perfect Bridegroom. He is a Healer. He is Alpha and Omega. He is "I AM THAT I AM." He is our portion and our inheritance. He is our salvation and our shield. He is always with us. He is the resurrection and the life. He is the way, the truth, and the life. He is Jehovah Nissa—the God of victory; Jehovah Shalom—the Lord of rest and peace; Jehovah Rapha—the Lord your healer; Jehovah Jireh—the Lord your provider; Jehovah Raah—the Lord your shepherd. The God who keeps His promises.

In my life, I have seen that He is a God who has my future, and it is good. He is a God I can trust. He is a God who loves me with a 1 Corinthians 13 love. He is not only worthy of being my Bridegroom but was destined to be my Bridegroom. His place in my heart was always meant to be the lover of my soul. The one who leads me. The one who already has my victory for me. The one who is fighting my battles. He is the God who lovingly fought for my heart and waited for me to choose to let Him in. He chose and loved me first. He walks with me by green pastures and gives me rest. I do not have to do anything to earn His love. I do not have to beg Him in my prayers. It is already done. He has already given me all that I need. I am not in want; I already have it. I just must believe it and walk in His time and His will. He is a God who left the ninety-nine to find me. He is a God who has all the answers and is not silent. He tells me my future and it is secure. I must just have faith and believe it is true. My circumstances no longer get to define me. My Bridegroom gets to define my circumstances. He is my leader. He leads me perfectly. He is perfect and never changes. He is consistent and knows exactly what I need. He is bigger than my faults. Bigger than my idols. Bigger than my lies. That is why He took all of them from me and replaced them with His love, truth, and goodness. He is mine, and I am His. How lucky am I to be the bride of Christ. To walk in victory every day. To laugh without fear of the future. To live each day as its own and let tomorrow worry about itself. I get to stay in the present with Him because my life is not my own. It is His. I just must listen and obey. I have been fighting my own battles my whole life, thinking I was God's warrior. I missed the point. Being a warrior is just saying "yes and amen" to Him. He will lead and win the battle for His victory. I just must listen. I no longer feel rejection, shame, or revenge. My God says that I am loved, I am worthy, I am beautiful, and I am His. My job as His bride is to love and to be loved, to not let others define me or control me, but to love. I am free because I surrendered all to God. I am living in victory. I am the chosen. I am loved. I am worthy. I am the bride of Christ. When you read these blogs, I hope you see the result, that you see this is not about me and never has been. This is and will always be about Christ, who lives in me. It is about how I finally gave Him permission to take over and how He made me beautiful from the ashes of my prison. He changed me from broken into whole. I am not perfect, but the One who has control of my heart is. If you look at me, you will see the flaws and mistakes. If you look at *Him in me*, you will see the greatest love story of all time.

I love you all, and I am rooting for your victory. The love story God has for you will be unique and beautiful. The result will be the same. God is who He says He is. He has your victory for you. He has your freedom. Will you let Him write your story, too?

THE ONLY WAY IS THROUGH

I went through a year of healing and surrender, and God broke out of the very small box that I had been keeping Him in. Although it was difficult, it was the best year I had ever had. In my deepest heartache and pain, I came face to face with the real God, and He was not the God I had imagined Him to be or the God the church teaches about.

On that New Year's Day, after another wrestling match with God, He told me something that changed my life. He said, *"My bride, the only way for your heart to be transformed is to walk through your pain with Me by your side."* Over the next two months, I locked myself in my house, isolating myself from my friends and family. I turned my phone off, I lost weight, and I avoided focusing on my outward appearance. I was not afraid of being alone. I spent my time allowing God to uncover all my lies, my pain, and the side of myself that I considered bad. I came face to face with the Healer. I could finally grasp the truth of who God is. This precious time enabled me to stop worrying about religion and the law, and it empowered me to step into a real relationship with the Lover of my soul. I knew that pretending my journey was complete and that I was healed would be a lie. I was on a roller coaster the whole time. I spent most of my days fighting God and discovering that God doesn't want perfection. He wants my heart. He wants willingness to change.

God made big promises to me. I was reluctant to write out the one that was most important to me. I told God, "If this doesn't come true, it will break me. Don't tell me it will come true, and then it does not." To develop my ability to hear God more clearly and step out in faith, I started keeping a prophetic journal.

Along with the prophetic journal, I started a daily hope journal to help build my hope in God's promises. As time passed, it seemed that my most treasured promise was going to come true and that God was sending me a husband. I met a man who said God told him he was the fulfillment of my promise.

My prophetic journal had several entries on how God was going to fulfill His promise and how great it would be. I finally surrendered my promise to God with a genuine heart. Then, in walks a man saying he is my promise. Of course, I fought it, but God convinced me the promise was real. I got excited, and I had hope. Wow! Look what God does when you listen to Him! This new man in my life and I prayed together the whole time. I asked my prayer partners to agree with us, too, and everything seemed to be a green light. Like all relationships, there were growing pains, but I trusted God to take care of them.

However, secretly, behind closed doors, I was a mess. I was insecure. I was not happy. I was irrational. One day, my promise walked away. I did not understand why. I felt like I was in limbo, I was angry, and I didn't understand why. Three thoughts entered my mind: (1) I don't hear from God (even though every other promise was answered), (2) God is a liar who tricked me and does not keep His promises, and (3) God was asking me to trust Him because He was doing something amazing behind the scenes to give me a great testimony. My prayer partners and I believed God was doing something amazing. Then one week turned into one month, and one month turned into two. This was not looking like what I thought it would. This caused an internal war, and I have been in that war ever since.

In the two months that I was at war with who I thought God is and who the Bible says God is, I had to revisit past trauma and un-healed wounds I thought had already been restored and made new. However, I discovered they were never healed. I had just covered them up. I had never chosen to go through my pain before. Instead, I used physical and emotional addictions and control to conceal my pain. This two-month period had been a mixture of torment and healing.

Please don't judge me too harshly when I talk about what I had to go through. I want to be real and open here. I have been vulner-able because I am not the only one dealing with these issues. I am not the only Christian questioning their faith or the character of God. I don't feel like we talk about this enough in the church.

There are so many hurting people who are too scared to question God and/or those around them. There are many who don't know how to have a relationship with anyone, especially with God. The truth is my questioning the character of God and wrestling with Him is the only way that I was able to find truth. I am not saying it is the best way for everyone. There are people who believe God is afraid to deal with their junk, and He will strike them dead if they question Him or admit they are angry with Him. This is why Chris-tians walk away from God and church. God is not afraid of your junk. He is not afraid of or offended by your anger. He is not afraid of you questioning His character and expanding your knowledge of Him. Even when I was angry and yelling at the top of my lungs, God never yelled back at me. Even when I doubted His goodness, God never got angry with me. He always assured me of His love for me and answered my questions.

Nevertheless, I thought about walking away. It took honest dialogue with God and talking to others to heal from my pain. I even watched movies about how others dealt with struggles and pain. All these things helped me come to terms with my hidden pain and trauma. Each of us is unique, and we need to keep looking until we figure out what works for us. Please, church, I am *begging* you, when you meet people in pain, don't give a "Christianized" answer. Listen to them. Let them know you hear them and pray for them. Perhaps you can tell them about your own healing experience.

When you are dealing with the desires of your heart and the fulfillment of God's promises that you've been praying about for years, the last thing you want to hear someone say is, "Well, God will use it for His good." Those kinds of statements can cause more pain. They can cause hurting people to think God is not good, and it may be best for them to run away. That is not how to help people who are hurting. The most difficult thing for me to do is talk about the pain I had to walk through before getting to my healing, but I am going to do that in the following paragraphs.

On this journey, I discovered various versions of myself. These were versions that helped me cope with past trauma and pain. The first one I came across was *suicidal Rachael*. Her re-emergence was distressing because I thought I had taken care of her sixteen years ago. She was just hidden by the alcohol or drugs that numbed my pain when she tried to show up. I struggled with intense pain while figuring out who God is, why He would lie to me, and why my faith was so weak. In my weakened state, I found myself struggling with suicidal thoughts. I wondered, *How did I get back here?* I knew I needed help, but before I could get it, *five-year-old mo-*

lested Rachael showed up. I was not aware of her because she had been buried deep within my subconsciousness. She had been trying to protect me for years. She was like a controlling five-year-old on steroids. Her way of protecting me was to control everything around me. She was the source of my need to control my environment and everyone who entered it. When I tried to defuse her by bringing her healing, she just kept yelling at me to leave her alone. I tried to get rid of her but was so numb after several failed attempts that I knew I needed help. I finally realized I had choices and saw that God could protect me. I started to recognize that I did not have to let my emotions control me, and I chose to stop acting out of unfounded radical emotion. Admittedly, I am not perfect, and sometimes I don't make my highest choice. However, I am walking in an elevated level of healing, and *suicidal Rachael* went away when *molested Rachael* was taken care of.

I experienced freedom until I decided to invite God into my heart as my Bridegroom. *Five-year-old Rachael* showed up again! No one had ever made it to my heart like this, and she was there waiting. After wrestling with God for a little while, I decided to give the *five-year-old* permission to rest and let God take over. Again, I had peace for a little while until I met *self-harm Rachael*. This was a tricky Rachael to deal with because *self-harm* was hidden within me for many years. *Self-harm Rachael* did the greatest harm through self-sabotage, drinking, or causing harm in other ways. Now that all the other addictions had been taken care of, *self-harm* showed up in all her fury. This scared me because I thought she had been healed a while ago. I did not want to deal with her because I was exhausted, full of emotional pain and physical fatigue. I did not come this far to go backward, so I prayed, and boom, she was gone.

At this point I really hoped no more *"bad" Rachaels* would show up. I was so exhausted. The next day, I felt someone tap my shoulder. I clenched my fist, and I got ready for a fight. I thought, *Oh no, I don't want to do this anymore. I am so exhausted. But okay, God, I promised I would walk through my pain with You, so here we go.* I turned around to come face to face with God. I looked at Him, and He said, *"Rachael, I am all that is left in your heart. Will you accept Me?"* I melted. All these years, all I wanted was God, but I had so much pain that I refused to walk through, and here He was asking for me to choose Him. I cried as I said yes, and I had peace like I had never had before.

I wish I could end the story here, but I still had to walk through a few more things. It is a continuing journey, and the next part is the most important part. I was struggling with understanding why I was so angry with God. I knew the anger was based on a lie, but the reality of my circumstances and past said otherwise. All I had ever known was a false reality clouded in pain. God kept saying to accept His love. I kept saying, "If You love me so much, why do I hurt all the time? How do I accept Your love? Why did You take away my promise? Do You love men more than women? Why do You let them get away with everything while we sit here praying for them and waiting on them to change their prideful hearts? Are You a good leader? Can I trust You? Right now, I want to know You, but I can't get past my hurt."

I was watching a Christian documentary that talked about God being a relational God and how He doesn't let our junk keep us from His love. He just wants to meet us where we are and have a relationship with us. I have heard this a million times, but this time, something hit me differently. I questioned whether I had a personal relationship with God. I rationalized to myself that I fasted and honored God and that I searched for Him. However, I had to examine if I was walking naked and unashamed with God in the Garden. Have I been eating from the tree of knowledge, consumed with good and evil? That was not how God designed me to be. He designed me to have a relationship with Him. At this moment I said something that has changed the direction of my life. "God, I choose to accept Your love, to accept You as You are, and have a relationship with You. I want to know You. Search my heart and clean me of all my lies." Oh, man! There are those powerful prayers again. As a result, I am on a different path and journey.

I have learned that the most beautiful thing about God is you can tell Him anything. I have hidden for years. Here is the truth: when you are introduced to sexuality at the age of five, you have no way to comprehend what that means. A five-year-old mind cannot understand sexuality because a five-year-old is meant to be innocent. Satan took his opportunity to pervert my mind at a young age. I did not know how to tell anyone about it. The perverted sexuality caused me to feel shame and guilt, and so I hid what I was thinking. I hated my thoughts. I hated how I did not want to think the things I thought. I had surrendered sex to God for ten years, but I was thirty-four years old, and I still had shame as if I was out there continuing to give my body away. I learned to hide from people and from God. I developed a need to be perfect in all things. It consumed me. It destroyed me.

As God healed me, I decided to not hide anymore. The fighting, the pain, and the roller coaster that I had been on for such a long time almost destroyed me and my relationship with God. I decided to give God free access to all my dirty, shameful, painful secrets. You know what He did? He purified me. He wasn't ashamed of those secrets. He wanted to transform them into something beautiful. He made them into His testimony in me. God cares about every little part of me. He cares about every small detail. He made me. He breathed life into me. He wants all of me. I had to let Him break out of the box I had built around Him so He could heal me. In two months, He healed me and answered three years' worth of prayers. Imagine what He can do now that I am surrendered to His will in me.

During this part of my journey, I learned that the most beautiful gift from God is having choices and taking every thought captive. God does not want prisoners. He wants you to give Him your free will so He can restore you. I have learned that freedom is the only solution. The Freedom Journey is always easy with God by your side. When I wake up every morning, I get to make a choice. Do I want to let God lead me, or do I want to take control? Do I trust God and have faith that He will make everything beautiful in my life? I can choose to not let my emotions control me. I can choose to go to God's Word and live from that instead of what my physical eyes see. Now, when I have emotions that tell me to give up or that something is not fair, I choose to read the Word and proclaim the Scriptures. I have decided to not choose the roller coaster. I also choose not to run to other people to get their opinions. Everyone has good intentions, but they are not God. His thoughts are higher than ours, and He knows what He is doing. I choose to believe Him even when it does not make sense to me. I can choose to let my thoughts wander in the direction of the enemy, or I can take each thought captive and give it to God. I can have outrageous faith. I used to say I did not have very much faith. I prayed for more faith (yeah, I should have known where that would lead). The truth is I always had faith. However, I usually put that faith in the enemy's hands. You have faith because you always believe in something—either God's plan or the enemy's plan. It's your choice who you want to put that faith in. I recommend God's plan. Trust me, this struggle would have been a lot easier and shorter if I had put my faith in God in the first place.

I also learned to merge my will with God's will. Therefore, the only will that is left in me is God's. This is also a choice. I wake up every day and say, "God I choose to follow Your will and not my own today." I repeat this throughout the day. God has had me do several interesting things, and I may never know why, but I must believe it is to show His love to one of His children. God's nature only allows for one thing, and that is love. Love is God's true nature, and to choose His will is to choose love. It also means it is in my best interest to choose His will in my life. This life is no longer my own; it is God's. What a relief to no longer feel the need to fight my own battles, to worry about tomorrow, or to control something I never had control of anyway. The most beautiful thing that I have learned is God loves people no matter what emotional state we are in. God always talks to me, and no matter what kind of emotional state I am in, He sends people to love me and speak His truth to me. He literally guided every step of my healing.

I just read something about surrender and forgiveness from inner vows. I made a list of inner vows I have made throughout my life and discovered I had made about 500 of them. I realized those vows kept me from God's will for my life. A friend encouraged me to join them in reading a book, and it took us ten weeks more to read it than it should have. However, I read that book at the exact time I was supposed to. God is so good. He knows exactly how and when to walk you through things. His way is loving, His yoke is easy, and His timing is perfect.

God reminded me about a blog I wrote years ago about my dog, Tebow. It was perfect for my situation at this time. I encourage you to read the blog I wrote called "How God Used a Dog to Show Me His Love." Over a two-month period, God took His very broken, angry, and exhausted daughter, and He healed her. I had been praying for years for freedom that only took Him two months to manifest in me. I had to be willing to admit I was broken. I had to stop hiding and be honest and real with Him. I had to yell. I had to fight. I had to be a completely wild person (I can't believe my neighbors did not call the cops with all that yelling. I already know my dogs think I am crazy). When I was at the end of myself, God was there. He was waiting for me. His hands opened wide. He just wanted to love me. He just wanted to heal me. He just wanted a relationship with me. I had been yelling at Him and blaming Him, and all He wanted was me. He wanted me in my imperfect state. I will never understand why, but I know God has a heart for the broken. He has a special love that heals all wounds. He does it in His own unique way. I had been praying for a miracle and it turns out the miracle is me. I get to be the main character in His love story. What a blessing and honor it is to be the bride of Christ, to be a daughter of the King.

I don't care how broken you think you are or how unworthy you feel. I don't care what you have done or how many people you have hurt. I don't care if you feel you have nothing to offer. Understand this one thing: God thinks differently than you do. God loves you. God wants you. God has a story for you. He wants you to be the main character in His love story that He wrote uniquely for you. I don't care how dirty you feel or how broken you are. God's love for you is bigger than anything you have said, done, or felt. As God heals you, His story in you will touch others. Don't let your brokenness keep you from the greatest love, freedom, or healing you will ever know. There is no situation God can't fix or heal. Just let Him in. Walk through your pain with Him to find His heart. Try not to fight Him so hard, but if you do, you might lose weight in the process!

I love you and appreciate you taking the time to read this. I am here for you. As you have seen, I have been through a great deal in my life, so nothing will scare me away from loving you and praying for you.

WHERE THE HURT
AND THE HEALER COLLIDE:
A JOURNEY INTO HOPE

God directed me to go to a specific place for a healing walk. As I planned it out, a big snowstorm hit the area. It was supposed to be a horrible day, and everyone was telling me to reconsider. I prayed and prayed, but God still gave me a specific day and area He wanted me to go. So, I packed extra water, food, and warmth, and I headed out alone with my two dogs on a somewhat intimidating journey.

At first, the roads were clear, and everything seemed to be going smoothly. Then I hit a snowy road, but I wasn't panicked because there were two four-wheel drive vehicles up ahead, clearing the snow for me. Then they turned off the road, and I was on my own. As I stayed on this snowy road, I started to notice that I was now driving over virgin snow. I had to make some turns and the snow was getting deeper. I could see familiar landmarks but still had not reached my destination. My heart started to race as I realized I was all alone in an area that did not feel safe and without cell phone reception.

As I made another turn, thinking that I was there, I realized I still was not there. At this point I did what I do best—I yelled at God, "I don't want to go any further. I can't do this. I am scared.

Where are You? Why did You send me out here?" Just as I was about to really lose it, I could hear God telling me to trust Him. The next thing I knew, I was there! As I stepped out of my car, I realized that my jeep was more than capable of managing the snow I had driven through. From this perspective, I could see I was never in danger. I was just looking at it from a different point of view in the car as opposed to outside of it. I could hear God say to me, *"Rachael, your perspective is off. Every time you feel like you can't see where you are going or feel afraid, you tell Me you don't want to do it and are frightened. Daughter, don't you see, you are almost there. You just can't see beyond the curve. Just go a little further and trust Me. It is not as bad as it seems."* I laughed because God always knows the right way to talk to me.

We walked and we talked. I was very aware of how alone I was. I was very aware of the fact that anyone could just grab me, and it would be game over. It was windy and cold, and I was uncomfortable. However, I also noticed the beauty of my surroundings. How still and quiet it was. How the air was fresh. How easy it was to hear God out here with no distractions, traffic noises, cell phones, or, for that matter, anything. I noticed how small I felt in such a big area. It was beautiful and frightening at the same time. It was thrilling and uncomfortable at the same time. It basically summed up the last three months of my life and the healing adventure I had been on. I am getting ahead of myself. Let's explore why I went out there in the first place.

For three months, I noticed that my faith seemed to be on sinking sand. I was very frustrated because while my heart was willing, I just couldn't seem to stay on the rock of the truth of God. Months before, I began to earnestly examine the lies I believed. Everything seemed to be going great, and I believed that after ten years of praying, God was going to give me all my promises (the image of driving on the road with snow mentioned above). Then, the journey got rocky, and I was hurting. I felt like God had lied to me, but I still had prayer partners speaking into my life and giving me their perspective on God's guidance (the snowy road with the four-wheel drive vehicles). Then suddenly, all my prayer partners were just getting blanks, and God told me it was time for me to walk through the healing with Him alone (the lonely, snowy road with all the curves and no tracks).

The problem with doing this alone was I did not trust that I heard from God. Sure, I could hear from God for *other* people, but when it came to my own life, I wasn't so sure. God has given me signs to tell me I am hearing Him, but my pain was bigger to me than His signs. Trying to have true faith in Him for the first time in a sensitive area (the most sensitive area in my life) but then not seeing it happen was reinforcing my doubt in God. I was unglued. One minute, I was experiencing truth and breakthrough, then I would lose it and be fighting God again. One day, I just cried as I told God He could take it all, "God, take all the lies, take all the hurt, take away my cloud of pain. I can't do this anymore. I can't stand on sinking sand anymore. I can't see you through my cloud of pain any longer. You can break me, God, so I am only left with You." Wow! Me and my dangerous prayers!

All God needs is a willing heart, and He can perform miracles. Five weeks later, and after another breakdown, I heard God speak to me, *"Rachael, get a piece of paper. It's time to remove your cloud of pain. I want you to listen to Me and write down everything that I tell you."* He told me about twenty-one areas of my life in which I believed lies. I began working in all these areas with Him. It wasn't easy. I woke up every day resisting the pain.

However, I was serious with God. I was willing to go through the pain to experience the release and breakthrough. I wanted to know God. I wanted unshakable faith. I wondered how people lose children but still love God and not question their faith. How did Stephen get stoned and, in the middle of his pain, ask God to forgive them? How did Daniel walk into the lion's den without kicking and screaming about how unfair it was?

To be super honest with you, I did not have faith like that. So, every day, I woke up in pain, pressed in, and walked through it with God. It was God and I and no one else. He was the perfect counselor. He healed me. He showed me the lies, and He disputed them with the truth from the Bible. Things really did happen and were painful and not fair. Those were harder to walk through, but God gave me a choice. I could choose to forgive and realize these things were never what He intended for me. He showed me that if I walk in His will, then I don't have to worry about it happening to me again. On the day of that snowy, cold walk, I revisited a very painful area of my life. I needed God to come in and heal me. I needed Him to meet me in a special place and heal what had been broken. I was seeing God through a broken mirror and what was being reflected to me was *not* who He was. I did not trust Him to lead me, I did not respect Him, and I felt like I had to protect myself from Him. Without going into detail, I had my reasons. I was unaware that I believed all these things until God revealed them to me. Again, I was left with a choice: Choose God's truth or live out of the lies I had been believing for over thirty years.

Here is what I learned. To begin with, I learned that I have a choice. God does not want slaves. He wants us to willingly seek Him. My perspective was off. I had to be willing to admit my trespasses, apologize, and forgive. The day of the walk, I went to my dad's house and apologized for some seriously bad things that I did as a child. This affected our relationship, and it affected the way I saw God. What amazed me was his response: "I just remember you being a very good kid, and I enjoyed you." I was in shock because this was not how I remembered it. I guess my dad changed his perspective. He made a choice. He *chose* to remember the good things about me. He *chose* to give me unconditional love no matter what I had done or what I thought I had done.

When I went on the walk, I kept thinking about my dad's reaction. He chose to just remember the best parts of me so he could give me unconditional love. That was so profound to me. As I finished up my walk, I saw a familiar area. As I went over to that area, memories came flooding back to me. Memories of happier times, a day in which I had so much hope. I was so excited, and promises were made that have now been broken. I started to weep. "Why God? Why would You bring me back here? We were doing so well until You brought me here to remember these broken promises and broken dreams." I heard God very clearly say, *"Rachael, you can remember all the bad things in this relationship and others, or you can be like your dad. You can choose to remember the good times and change your perspective so you can have unconditional love in this area."* Right there in the middle of the cold snow with no one around, alone, uncomfortable, brokenhearted, and weeping, I said, "Okay, God. I choose to remember only the good things and forget the bad. I choose to believe Your promises. I don't see the whole picture, and I choose to let You restore my broken relationships." I left that snowy, familiar, beautiful place of broken dreams, a different person. I left the old Rachael behind. I made a choice to let go of my anger, my need to be right, and my pain and let God restore the brokenness in me. It is not about being right. It's about loving people.

During this whole process, I have been seeking God in a different way and reading a lot of things to help my emotional and spiritual growth. The main thing I learned from all the readings is that your emotions are real, and you should acknowledge them. However, they don't have to control your actions. Several times during this process, I have given in to my emotions, and those days are always the days I end up fighting God. However, more and more, I am choosing to *not* act on my emotions. Let's face it: in an hour or so, I will have different emotions anyway. Instead of thinking or speaking into my negative emotions and giving them power, I decided to do praise and worship instead. In a real relationship with God, it's not always about what I feel like doing. Feelings can be deceiving and lead us into a number of pitfalls if we let them. It's about being obedient to God. It is about doing what His Word says. It's about being still and listening to His voice and directions.

I can try to fight my own battles. In fact, for most of my life, I *tried* to fight my own battles. I discovered it only makes me tired, emotional, and a hot mess. I usually end up going back and doing it God's way after I have completely failed on my own. Now, I engage in praise and worship, still myself, and surrender to Him. If I am upset, I still go out and have fun with my friends. I don't surrender to my feelings, and I choose to have fun. Guess what? When I have fun, my feelings change. I'm not saying to ignore your feelings. I did that for years, and that is why I am on this journey. However, you should not act on every single emotion you have and give power to it.

Let God fight your battles. Praise Him, wait for Him, and then act when He tells you what to do. That way, you are not exhausted, defeated, and angry. If He says pray and you don't feel like it, do it anyway. If He says forgive, but you don't think they deserve it, forgive anyway. It's not about what you want. It's about building such a strong relationship with God that you know His voice. At first, it will not feel good, but you will find that instead of the whole day being ruined by your emotions, only one or two hours might be bad, and the rest of your day is great. Each day, I pray, "God, give me all that I need." I discovered that if I do not get something today, it is because I don't need it today. Either you believe God is good and that He gives you all you need, or you don't believe He can or will. I attest to this because deep down inside that is what I believed for many years. The truth is, He always gave me *exactly* what I needed. I always thought I was missing out on something more and was never satisfied. I lived from my emotions and not His will.

Staying in God's will can be hard for me. I am used to making my own decisions and protecting myself. I honestly did not have a clue how to stay in His will. So, I asked Him. Then I started asking Him about everything. God went over twenty-one areas of my life to remove lies and replace them with the truth. I asked Him about my future marriage. I asked Him what my marriage should look like. I asked Him about my future children and their legacy. I asked Him what He meant when He said, *"I dare you to dream again."* You name it, and I asked it. I spent three weeks asking questions and listening to God. You know what? He was *always* there, and He *always* answered all my questions. He healed me in a way only He can. He is the perfect counselor. God healed areas of my life over a three-month period that could have taken years. It hurt so good, and it was amazingly beautiful. I have heard people say that they can't hear God and He is silent, but I have never known Him to be silent. When He appears to be silent is when:

1. I did not ask the right question.

2. I did not ask at all.

And/or:

3. I didn't like His answer, and I didn't respond, which resulted in Him waiting until I did what He said.

I don't believe God is silent. I believe He is vulnerable and relational. He wants us to be honest with Him and allow Him into every area of our lives. God cares about every intimate detail of your life. When I looked past my pain, I could see so many amazing things He has done in my life. For example, my dogs are a gift from God. He gave me my family and friends to help me through this time. When the pain got so intense and I cried out to Him, He guided me to books, movies, and music to help me. God is a God of relationship. His goal is healing your heart and having you know who He truly is.

To really get to know God as a relational God, I had to ask Him to break the curse of Adam and Eve. If, through Jesus, we can break generational curses in our family, then why can't we break the original curse? The curse of the knowledge of the tree of good and evil. The hardest thing for me to give up is my need to know. I asked God why I needed to give up my need to know. It didn't make sense. Don't I need to know how this will end? Don't I need to know if God is going to answer my prayer? What happens in your relationship with God when no one can answer your questions, and God is not answering them the way you want? What if you never get to know why you went through something? Will you still have faith? Will you still think God is good? I wrestled with these thoughts for a very long time. It almost caused me to walk away. One day, I decided to let it go and give it to God. I decided to have unshakable faith like Daniel or Steven. I needed to know God, meet Him in His Garden, and walk with Him daily. I was not created to need to know anything. I was created to have a stable relationship with God and trust Him. When I ask Him what His plan is for my life today, my job is to answer yes and amen to His responses. I can trust Him to lead me through my life while I rest and let Him fight my battles for me. I have fasted, I have prayed, I have lost weight, I have fought, I have cried, and the answer to all my pain was: "Let go and let God." God is restoring the shattered mirror through which I saw Him. I had to get to the end of me to let God fix the broken pieces of me. It was in the surrender that I came face to face with a God who wanted a relationship with me. A God who wanted to restore me. A God who said, *"My daughter, you are asking the wrong question. It is not 'Why'; it is 'Who.' Who do you say I am? Who do you think I am? Who is going to restore you?"* The rest falls into place. The biggest and hardest question I had for God was why the world is full of so much pain. I started looking for movies and books that talked about pain. Stories of people who did not deserve the pain they experienced. They did everything right, but still, life fell apart. You know, real-life Job stories. My doubt was killing me. I wondered if God loved me, why did He allow so much pain in my life? Some of it was because I wasn't listening to Him and not staying on His path. But there were times it was because of others' choices that affected me. I was innocent. I was young. My cry was, "Why did You not protect me? Why did You not want to give me the marriage You promised me and the children You said would be my legacy? I surrendered everything! I did everything You asked! I finally had hope! I finally listened to You! For the first time in my life, I trusted You and I got crushed! Am I crazy? Should I go to a psych ward because I think I hear from God? Are You teaching me a lesson by kicking me down when I just learned how to walk?" My doubts started to suffocate me. I began to question the character of God. I have been told my whole life not to doubt God. So now that I did, what did that mean? Am I a bad Christian? I read a book that said doubt is neutral. It is what you do with it that decides what it becomes. Doubt can be good. It was my doubt that pushed me out of a superficial relationship with God. It showed me that I believed lies about God. Doubt made me dig in deeper. It made me do research. It made me ask God to search my heart and know me. What did I find? Is there a magical answer to why God allows pain? Does everyone, in the end, get an amazing life after trusting God and surrendering? Yes and no. Children still die. Divorces still happen. Life still sucks sometimes. However, I learned that you get to make choices. You can live in that pain and get swallowed up by your grief, your doubt, and your pain. You may even have convinced yourself it is the right choice, but what kind of life is that? For me, I realized that there is no hope, joy, or love found outside of the Trinity. Without God, I literally have nothing. I heard Him say very clearly: *"Rachael, you have been running from pain for so long and trying everything to avoid pain. Your last protection method is pain. You choose to put yourself in pain before someone else can. I want you to surrender your pain to Me. Give it to Me. It is killing you. It is blocking the life I have for you. How can you love Me and choose pain? How can you know Me and choose pain? It is either accepting My love or choosing your pain. Which one is it?"* My response was to remind God that I still had not received His promise of marriage or kids. I still didn't know why things were happening like they were, and I didn't think it was fair. However, as I thought back on it all, I realized that what I did know was that my doubt pushed me to know God. I know that I now have an unshakable relationship with Him. I know He replaced my pain with His love, and I will never be the same. I know even when I am in pain, I choose to love others like He loves me. I know He will use my pain to help others. I know that I am not the same, and I would not change that for anything in the world.

In a book I am reading, a missionary tells villagers in a very poor country about Disneyland. Except this country has no word for *mouse* or *castle*. By the end of the story, the missionary was trying to explain the happiest place on earth, but the villagers interpreted that Disneyland is run by a witch-rat who lives in a hut doing evil things, and they vowed to never go there. Imagine these villagers' surprise if they ever got to go to the real Disneyland! The joy they would have when they discover it is a magical place. I feel like that is us when we try to interpret God's plan for our lives. Our perspective and life experience keep us from understanding what Disneyland looks like. It is not an evil rat doing witchcraft, but a magical place. On my hardest days, I imagine the vulnerability of the Trinity. The complete openness they proved for us. We think we are to do things alone. To be strong. To not involve others. In the meantime, the Trinity's example and what They desire is to be completely vulnerable. They don't need us, but They choose us. We can offer Trinity nothing, but They offer us everything. They invite us to sit with Them at the table and accept Their never-ending flow of love for us. I imagine a faucet of Their love pouring into me. That faucet will never run out of love flowing into me. It is my choice to leave it on or turn it off. I hope I always choose to leave it on so I am so full of His love that it comes out of me and pours out onto everyone around me.

PAIN OR LOVE: WHICH WILL I CHOOSE?

God is love. Pain is from the enemy. I can't have both residing inside of me.

So, what will it be? Do I want a love that surpasses all understanding or a pain that just wants to lie to me? Do I want truth and peace to guide me or a pain that wants to eat up the inside of me?

I can't have both; I must choose.

Do I want a love that will fight for me or a pain that is dulling the light inside of me? A love that is willing to die for me, or a pain that is trying to hide from me. A love that is trying to save me, or a pain that is creating a grave in me. A love that is brave and creating grace in me, or a pain that is creating a slave out of me?

I must choose; I can't have both.

God can't reign in a heart full of pain. For Freedom is in His name but the enemy is full of shame. So, I must choose: is it Love or Pain, God or the enemy, to whom my heart lays claim?

CAN YOU RESTORE WHAT IS LOST?

"Can You heal a broken heart, God? Can You restore a childhood that has been lost? Can You fix a wound so deep I can't see You from way down there? Can You make me believe that fathers care? That love doesn't come from pain?

"A childhood missing is hard to repair. Is it gone forever, and can You restore it by turning back time? Can You love me from way up there? A broken image coming from a broken mirror. Is there hope that You can repair it?

"Can You heal all the time I did this alone? No husband by my side to wipe away the tears I have cried. I have waited for ten years.

"Can You replace a child's cry that I cannot hear, for he is not there? No child to hold or call my own. God, can You make up for that lost soul? A promise You give, but there is no end in sight.

"God, can You change my bitter and angry heart?

"I want to embrace You as You call me, but instead, I draw back with a smack, ready to fly from me. God, can You change this defensive heart?

"Is it true I don't need to protect myself when all I have known is pain and brokenness? How can I believe You are good when even You won't give me what You promised?

"Do You really love this broken mess? Will I ever get where You want me to be? Can You, yes You, even fix me? Can You take what has been stolen and make it new? All this precious time wasted; can You make up for it? God, can You really give it back better than before?

> *"Can I really trust You? Are You better than the men in my life who come to destroy? Can You protect me without breaking me first? Can I really have hope? Hope is so deceiving and seems to break me. God, can You fix this broken woman who is called me?"*
>
> *"My daughter, yes, I can and will fix your broken heart. I Am renewing you and restoring what was lost. Yes, I Am giving back your childhood. You will experience it fully restored with your children.*
>
> *"Yes, My daughter, I will restore you piece by piece. Better than you were before. I don't have to turn back time. My hope is in the right now. Right now, I Am by your side. I Am waiting for your embrace. I know your heart is breaking, and you are having trouble letting go.*
>
> *"I Am waiting by your side. I Am right here waiting for you.*
>
> *"I don't rush or demand things to happen at a certain time. But you do, My daughter. Don't you see My timing is perfect? My will is set.*

Your husband, you will get. In fact, you already know him. You already love him.

"Hold on to My promise, for it is true. No, time has not been lost. Your marriage came at a cost that was paid, but the price was worth the wait. You will cry tears of happiness when you see what I have already made for you. A child is coming, actually, two. One is already formed and here waiting for you. There have been no souls lost. Instead, I have worked on yours so theirs can be saved.

"There is no lost time, but time is restored.

"Hang in there, My daughter; it is all on the way. Hope and faith are necessary for this walk. Stop chasing pain. Freedom is My name. My daughter, will you wait? Will you trust Me? Will you claim My name over this situation? I will restore everything, for nothing is lost. Hope is in My name. To know hope is to know Me.

"So, what will you choose, My daughter? Will you choose Me?"

CAN HOPE GROW
IN A BROKEN SOUL?

"God, can there be hope found in a broken soul? Can it replace a pain that is suffocating me? So heavy, sitting on my chest. I go to breathe, but it sucks the air out of me.

"Can it be? Is there a chance that with a little bit of faith, this broken soul can accept growth? When all I have ever known is fear and pain that keeps me stuck?

"I have run away from Your love for so long; is there still a chance for a romance? I feel all alone and buried in my pain. But could it be You placed a seed there? Deep in my heart that You watered with all my fallen tears.

"Is it true You won't leave me there, but instead, are You growing hope to lift me out of my own despair? Could it be I see You breathing your life back into me? I mean, are You really changing me?

"It's been so long since I have dreamed, but I can feel this hope growing inside of me. Please tell me that this little seed won't be crushed by all my fears and anxiety. Tell me what You grow is stronger than my doubts. But God, can it be, is it true that, in fact, the little seed is growing into hope that will save me?

"If I choose to let You water my seed instead of speaking into my pain, will You be able to heal me?

"Will this broken soul dare to have hope?"

A FATHER'S SHOULDERS

A father has a lot on his shoulders. He seems to carry the weight of the world, for the weight he carries is also his family's. His decisions affect their future. He must protect them physically, mentally, and emotionally.

He must listen to God and hear Him correctly. His own wants and desires are no longer his focus, for he must watch out for his family instead.

No father is perfect. No father is without blame. His decisions can't always be 100 percent correct.

We don't love you because you're perfect or always accurate. We love you because we see what you carry and what you sacrifice for us.

So, to the father whom I love, I want you to know when you took on too much and felt like you let us down, it's okay. We love you for who you are. Your love built us up, allowing us to become who we are.

I know it's a burden to always be in charge. I know you also carry your own scars. It's hard to heal when you take on more.

Dad, God always saw your heart.

Dad, don't let the enemy place too much on your shoulders, for I love you the way that you are. God made you perfect just for me.

Won't you let go of the weight you have carried? For too long, it has robbed your joy. For too long, it has stolen your peace. Dad, let God lift that load off your shoulders. For He died for you so He could carry all your burdens.

GOD'S FAIRY TALE

I want to believe there is something beautiful awaiting me in Your fairy tale. The way You pursue me and call me Your own.

I tried to pretend I was strong and bold. But truthfully, I was screaming for someone to save me. I created my own Babylon, full of counterfeits and wasted time. I was trying to keep myself busy and entertained. Heaven forbid I see what's really going on. A past that haunted me and kept me a slave. Men who destroyed me and used me for their own way.

Do You really have a fairy tale promised for me? Yeah, right, God, come on, please. With so much pain, who can believe? I was wasting away and dying because of everything inside of me. Could it be the best thing a man ever did was walk away so You could heal me?

A love story waiting to unfold. A God who came just to restore me as I broke into a million pieces on the floor. I had nothing left to hold onto. You put me back together, piece by piece, restoring me back to Your original design. You are making me Your masterpiece that all can enjoy for all time.

As I cried, you patiently caught all my tears. You stored them up for a story You will use later. No pain was wasted; nothing was lost. You used my pain and changed it to love. This was a necessary cost that You bought for me on the cross.

My anger and rage could have crucified You again. Each word and lie a nail hammered into Your hands and feet. Oh man, I just realized that could have been my fate. But You did not leave me there to suffer hate. Out of my mustard seed of faith, hope began to grow. I heard You say as clear as day, *"My daughter, it's not about why, when, how, or could you, but Who. Who do you say I am?"*

At that moment, a light broke through the darkness in my heart. It no longer was about the journey or the circumstance. It was about the One leading and guiding me to a glorious end. A choice He gave me in love that shined through all my pain. I could leave my past and walk into my restored future He had prepared without disdain.

No matter what I think is lost, He repairs, restores, and makes it new. All I must do is choose a future laid in victory. A will and time that is set for me.

It turns out the freedom was in letting go. Beautifully broken until nothing was left so He could breathe life, love, and hope back into me. A new creation set free. A perfect love story that He wrote just for me. A story that He will use and is meant to be told about how God came in and lovingly saved my soul.

His perfect bride, whom He loved, asking, *"Will you save this dance for Me?"*

GOODBYE TO MY OLD FRIEND

It's time to say goodbye to you, my old friend. You came in like a thief in the night. I was young, and you promised to take my pain. In my youth and innocence, I thought, *Hey, I mean, who wants pain anyway?*

Let's face it: you were never about being fair. You only care about destroying all that is near. You didn't care if it was right. You came to me at an age where I didn't know how to fight. Promises you made were like kisses sealed with death. You disguised yourself as a good friend. All the while, you were hiding your identity from me.

There was no room for anyone else. You became a safety net, encouraging me to jump. But you had no intention of catching me. Instead, you let me fall into your deep abyss of pain and torture. You whispered sweet lies to make me believe. I thought I needed you to survive. All the while, you were plotting to deprive me of everything.

You promised to protect me, but really, you just seek to kill, steal, and destroy. Pain became my only friend as you robbed me of all my joy. You made me think that taking pills was a good idea. Drowning my sorrows in alcohol was your solution to my downfall.

You laughed as you whispered in my ear, "Take that knife; it will help you, heal you, my dear." As you watched me bleed, you told me you loved me. How it made you laugh as you watched my life slowly fade away.

You told me I would have control if I let you lead. How strong I must be to not have emotions or let anyone in. You became my identity. What a fool I was to listen to you. But you were always there to drag me down. You never left my side as you pulled me to the ground.

I never had control; I was your slave. I didn't know I deserved so much more. God made me promises, but I couldn't partake with you as my sidekick, stealing it away.

God asked me to believe what He said about me was true, but dear old friend, you yelled louder than Him. Till one day, you pushed too hard.

God's light shone through and canceled out your darkness. I had a decision that was not easy to make. Choose a life full of pain with you, which was all I had ever known—a friend who robs me of myself. Or I choose God, who offers life, freedom, and hope.

So, goodbye, old friend, I don't need you anymore. God, my Father, bought me at a price. I am His daughter, so you must leave. You have no power over me. I tear up any contract I made with you in my ignorance. You offer no peace, just lies, death, destruction, and rage.

It's time I agreed with the Savior of the world and my soul. I believe His words and promises are true.

I became so used to you, and I believed it would hurt to kick you out. I thought I could never let you go. To be honest, I won't miss you at all. You are a liar and a counterfeit. Your promises only offer death.

My God is resurrection and life. His promises will restore all you stole. I will walk in victory and hold onto the promises He gave to me. I do believe everything He says about me. I was so much more than you said I was. I guess the power of God in me scared you more than I thought it would.

So, don't you see, you kiss of death? I don't need or want you anymore. My Father gave me life in just one breath. You're a liar and a cheat. He is my life.

So, goodbye, my enemy, because you're no friend to me. You're not welcome here anymore. I choose to live my life for the Savior of my soul.

LIVING FOR COUNTERFEIT OR TRUTH

Warning: This blog is not written for the weak of heart. This is the most vulnerable I have ever been and is meant as an expression of healing. The purpose is to help those who have been broken and need the Trinity to put them back together. I invite you to take a journey with me as God puts back the broken pieces that were called me. A journey in which I died to myself and was restored and made new in Christ.

People ask why people want to commit suicide. "How can they be so selfish?" Well, as someone who has had three failed attempts at suicide and has considered it multiple more times, I can only tell my story. Maybe it will bring insight to some and *healing* to others.

In retrospect, maybe attempts at suicide were selfish acts. At the time, I could not think about anyone but myself. I just wanted the pain to stop. I never thought I was going to hurt anyone. In fact, I really did think that the world and everyone around me would be better off without me in it. I have recently walked through all the lies and deceptions of the enemy. The enemy attacked my mind with suicidal thoughts at a young age when I was innocent and naïve. One small, seemingly innocent thought can turn into three suicide attempts, hospital visits, and years of intense therapy that didn't get to the root of the problem anyway. So how does a young, successful, Christian woman with a seemingly happy childhood get to this point? Well, life isn't always what it seems.

I thought I had an amazing childhood. Unfortunately, I could not remember any of it. At the beginning of my season of healing, I started reading a book by Joyce Myers called *Beauty from Ashes*. I was very confused because she had been severely abused as a child. The way she acted and managed emotions was almost exactly like the way I did. I remember talking to my friend during our walk one night and saying, "I mean, I was molested, but what other abuse did I have?" Being molested did not seem like that big of a deal. Kids are kids, and a certain girl decided to experiment with me when I was five years old. She was about nine years old. So, how could that be a big deal? It turns out that if you can't remember your childhood, there is a reason. The first step was acknowledging I had been sexually abused and that it was a big deal. Then, I could begin dealing with my "Bad Rachael."

When I thought I was finally healed, the real journey began. I started to remember my childhood. It was not as cheery or perfect as I thought it had been. I started reading my old diary. At eleven years old, I made an innocent (not so innocent) statement, "God, I wish I was in heaven with You. There is so much pain here on earth, and I really don't like or enjoy my life." What followed in the diary were years of making horrible mistakes, drinking, and self-harming, and it ended when I was eighteen with my suicide note.

An innocent statement is a foothold for Satan to step in, and he only does one thing: steal, kill, and destroy. I spent years believing lies that no one could be trusted. I believed I was unlovable and that I would never change. I experienced guilt about trying to be a good Christian while struggling with my addictions. In the diary, there were fantasies about dying that started at the age of eleven. It seemed the only dreams I had were to escape the pain and to go to heaven. Why did an eleven-year-old want to die? My greatest curse in life was that everything that happened to me seemed to not be bad enough to be exposed, but at the same time, it was not normal.

When I was five years old, I learned how to hide my pain, protect myself, and manipulate others to think I was okay. I became skilled at not being bothered by bad things that happened to me. I learned the phrases "It's no big deal" and "I am okay; nothing can hurt me." Before I turned eighteen, I had experienced molestation, rage, enabling, co-dependency, violence, physical abuse by men, bullying, sexual abuse, alcoholism, self-harm, pill-popping and overdosing, being cheated on, multiple suicide attempts, and drug addictions. I guess you could say I was selfish for trying to commit suicide, but I also thought there was no other way out from my pain. My mind had been conditioned by the enemy from the time I was eleven to believe that suicide and escaping to heaven was the only way to stop that pain. What was the point of living if this is all, you know?

I was very sick as a child. I had a disease that the medical community was not able to diagnose. I was extremely underweight and in pain the majority of the time. I ran high fevers and got sent home from school a lot. I also had multiple surgeries. By the time I was five years old, I learned to stop crying and embrace the pain to survive. I remember being eight and throwing up before school. I hid it from my parents because I was tired of being sick and wanted to go to school. I made a vow that day that I would control the pain. I ignored the pain and made it go away by making the pain feel somewhat good.

Even when I was eight, I could feel the Holy Spirit warning me that this was wrong. I was tired of pain and being sick, so I ignored the Holy Spirit. To be fair, I don't think I understood what the Holy Spirit was at that age, but I knew what I was doing was wrong. I have known for a long time that I have a problem with pain. I have been accused of putting my body through bad things to make my goals happen. I have been told by so many doctors that ignoring symptoms could have resulted in severe issues. In addition to it causing physical damage, it caused me emotional and spiritual damage.

In one of my clinical rotations, when I was training to be a physical therapist, I read about a man who was into sadomasochism. He had polio as a child and was in constant pain. He had given his brain to science after he died. What they found is that the brain, which is very changeable, had rewired itself. Instead of neural pathways connecting pleasure to the normal areas of happiness and joy, it was connected to pain. Meaning his brain had rewired itself, so the only way he could feel pleasure was through pain. He had no choice; his brain was wired incorrectly. However, he had a choice. He just didn't recognize it. I am sure when he was young, he did what I did and chose to ignore pain and turn it into pleasure so he could survive. God told me that is what I did as a child, too. I was in a situation where He was telling me to have faith, but even though He had shown me so many signs and miracles, I continued to choose pain. I learned to choose pain over love. I chose the enemy's plan over God's because my brain needed to be rewired so that pain no longer brought pleasure. In my childhood, cutting always felt good to me because my brain was wired opposite of how God had created my brain to operate. This is why suicide was such a tempting thought. The idea of pain brought peace and an escape from my reality. I realized at that point I could not remember the last time I was happy. It was when I was seven and before I made that inner vow. So silly that, as a child, you could cause so much harm. I asked God to rewire my brain, and He did. He is teaching me how to live life without pain.

Shortly after I wrote that last paragraph, God had me write a poem about me kicking out a pain demon. It turns out the inner vow I made when I was eight allowed a demon to come in. I agreed with that demon for almost thirty years. All because I did not want to have pain. I felt strong and proud that I could ignore the pain and push through. I thought it made me more valuable. What it did was destroy me physically, emotionally, and mentally. I had to choose God's love over the pain demon. I had to let God show me my identity as He designed it. Pain is from the enemy, and love is from God. You can't have both existing within you without a major inner conflict. You must choose which one you will listen to. I loved God.

I honored God, but God could not have full control of my heart with a pain demon protecting me and being my identity. The thing about demons is they can only kill, steal, and destroy. They never stop at just making you uncomfortable. This demon has been trying to kill me for years. He has done it slowly and painfully and has enjoyed watching me suffer. However, God's truth and character made it uncomfortable, and I chose God. Does that mean I feel pain now? Yes. Hiding the pain caused me to see it as normal and caused me to be immobilized and unable to heal, but experiencing pain through God's love is pushing me forward.

I was addicted to running away from pain. Perhaps we are all addicted to running away from our pain. The truth is I was addicted to controlling my own pain. I never wanted to be rejected, and I never wanted to be anything less than perfect. I did not want to go through the truth. I did not want to take time or spend emotional energy trying to heal. So, I ran, and I hid behind alcohol, drugs, pills, cutting, vacations, football, and multiple hookups. Then, I rededicated my life to God. I stopped all my addictions, or so I thought. Drinking was under control, but I had issues sometimes. I controlled my emotions because, again, I had to protect myself, and only "I" (or my pain demon) would put myself in pain.

I would not let anyone else come in and do that. Until one day, God made me a promise, and my promise came walking through the door. I was a mess. I was trying to let God and my promise in and let the pain demon go. I was physically abusive to myself behind closed doors, I hid my emotions, and I became a pretender. I knew I was not okay. I knew I could not hide or pretend forever. I knew God had to change me. Little did I know the way He would answer those prayers. My promise left. I was angry. I was so mad at God. I started on a process of embracing my pain and then rejecting it.

I wanted to go back to all my addictions. I wanted to harm myself. I wanted to randomly hook up with men; I wanted to move (run away). I wanted to do anything but face pain and deal with the things God needed me to heal from. I did not go this far to turn around, so I said let's do it. What followed was a very painful six months. I had to relive trauma I had not seen in thirty years. I had to embrace it. I had to admit it happened. I had to realize it was a big deal and it affected me and changed me. The hardest thing I had to admit was I did not have a childhood. I was so angry because I thought God had stolen everything from me. Why did I deserve this? The hardest part of this journey is what I am about to tell you. It is hard to admit you don't always have it figured out. I had a breakdown that I did not expect. Some issues triggered this breakdown and took me to a place I thought I would never visit again.

I don't know why I lost all hope when it happened, but I did. I went home, and I was angry. God had asked me a while before to ask Him the tough questions. He said this was going to be the hardest part. So, I asked. He told me I was mad at Him for lost time. A lost childhood and not being married in my thirties. I was mad because I would be an old mom. I was mad because I wanted to be married with kids eight years ago. I was also mad that He saved my life sixteen years ago if this was all my life was going to be. So that night, I came home. I yelled and said to God, "I am trapped. I can't get married. I can't have kids. I can't have sex. I can't even end my life. I am trapped. I don't want this life if I can't be happy. Everyone says I should be happy because I am success-ful, I travel, I have a great job, a great reputation, a lot of friends and people who love me, and I help a lot of people. I am still not happy. So, what's the point? I can't get back lost time. I can't get my childhood back. I can't be who You want me to be. I am tired. I have tried everything You have asked me to do, but even You don't love me. If You loved me, You would make up for these lost things. Here I am, weeks away from turning thirty-five and not one word from my promise. I can't and won't do this anymore." So, yes, I was again believing every lie Satan threw at me. But the lies felt so real. Let's face it: I have not wanted to live since I was eleven, so I guess you can say this was a long time coming. My suicidal tendencies never went away. Even two blogs back, I passed through it like it was not a big deal. I am over it. But with no addictions, no idols, not anything left but truth, it hit me hard again. I don't want to be alive. I have not wanted to live for most of my life. I can't be happy. I can't trust anyone. *I don't trust You, God.* So, I went into my sports room and lay down. I begged God:

"You have to intervene because right now, all I want to do is stop this pain. It has been twenty-four years of pain, more like thirty. If this is what my life is, then forget it. Why did You save me? Why would You love this mess? I can't even be who You want me to be. I can't be perfect enough for You. I just wrote on my Facebook how excited I was that it had been sixteen years since my last suicide attack, and here I am, a hypocrite." I started to look up on my phone to see if you will go to hell if you commit suicide. I also looked up scriptures to help with suicide. My phone kept sending me links to call the suicide hotline, but I knew only God could save me. As I lay there crying that night, trying to get my mind right, my dog, Tebow, came in and licked me and then lay by my side. I heard God's still small voice say, "My daughter, I am right here. I need you to fight. I can't do this for you, because you chose this at eleven. I will fight for you. I will show up. You will win. My daughter, fight." So, I read my last blog. Something in me just snapped, and I turned on KB and played "Armies." The next thing I knew, these words started flowing from my mouth: "I want to live. I am not eleven anymore. Satan, you dirty cheat, you can't have me! I tear up any contract I made with you when I was innocent. You have no power over me. I choose God's covenant; I choose life. I choose freedom. I choose Jesus." I started to see a vision. The light was pouring out of me, and Satan was being pushed back. I knew God had just kicked that stronghold out of my life, and I was finally free. The next day, I woke up happy to be alive for the first time since I was eleven. I have been happy to be alive every day since. That night was the most pain I had ever been in. Joy came in the morning, and I have had joy ever since. Not all days are perfect, but at least I value my life now. That day, when I asked God why I felt trapped and like the walls were closing in, his answer was beautiful. He said, "My daughter, you are right. You can't go to either side or back because the narrow path is only for My chosen. Few choose it because it is hard. Your flesh does not want to choose it because it hurts. My daughter, I am advancing you into My perfect will."

To answer your questions, yes, suicide is selfish, but it is complicated. A five-year-old has no way to emotionally grasp molestation, rage, alcoholism, sickness, pain, and a lost childhood. People feel sorry for the five-year-old but have no patience or love for the thirty-four-year-old who is still trying to protect themselves from a five-year-old mindset. They need God's love to transform them. My biggest downfall was that I was good at manipulating. I was good at hiding. I was good at making people think I was okay all the time. I even believed it myself. I was in shock when I had to find out all the trauma I had survived. I just found out recently that I tried to commit suicide because my boyfriend's friend sexually abused me in front of my boyfriend and our friends. We were all drunk, and no one knew he did it. I was too drunk to stop him. I had not dealt with my molestation when I was five, so I felt guilty. I felt like I deserved it. I felt like I did something to cause it. When I went to the hospital during the most embarrassing and traumatic moment of my life, while feeling exposed and vulnerable, I was treated badly. I told the MD that it was because I fought with my boyfriend. That is what I chose to believe. The MD yelled at me and made me feel like I was not even a human being. I felt like I deserved that too. So, when you see someone trying to commit suicide or cutting or performing self-harm, I want you to remember that there is always something hidden underneath. We were all just innocent five-year-olds at one time.

God gave me godly parents. They prayed for me. They loved me. They did their best, and it was enough to save me. I am grateful for my parents. They made mistakes, but who doesn't? I have talked to them. I have asked for forgiveness for my wrongs and have talked to them about the pain I believe they left in my life. God orchestrated the whole thing, and it was beautiful. There has been healing and there has been restoration. God is a good Healer and a good Counselor. He restores all that is lost. No pain has been wasted, and I am so grateful that He has used my life to help other people heal. It is a great gift to come out on the other side and be God's testimony. I know He has an amazing marriage and life for me. I can't wait to see all that He restores.

I know this blog is long, and I hope I have not lost you. So, let us talk about sex! Did I get your attention now?

I have been praying for a while for God to restore my sexual thoughts and tendencies back to His design. I had no idea what that meant. When you are introduced to sex at five years old, there is no way it can be healthy. A five-year-old has no idea how to manage that kind of information. I didn't get introduced to sex by a talk with my parents. I was introduced to it physically and without consenting to it. So, the enemy had a field day with it. I know that I was a slave to lust. Lust is a demon. It has no place in the life of a healthy adult.

After sexual abuse, molestation, and years of being lied to, I had no idea how to have a healthy sex life. Sure, I did Love Waits as a teenager. I really wanted to wait, but my mind was a battlefield. I was losing the battle to the enemy, and I was suffocating. Every time I had sex with someone, I never felt like it was my choice. To keep them, I felt like I had to have sex with them. Then, I used sex to escape pain and to manipulate. I could not have a healthy relationship with men due to my past pain and abuse. I could, however, get them to love me with sex, or so I thought.

Sex became a game. It was destroying me. It never fulfilled me. I always needed more, and then it left me empty. I couldn't find love in it. It was about an hour or so of freedom from the pain in my life. Lust was consuming me and destroying my relationships. It was keeping me in relationships that I should not have stayed in. It was sucking all the dignity and life out of me. For an hour or so, I felt the best release of pain and temporary joy, but then I felt shame and guilt. I repeatedly kept going back. I let men destroy me emotionally, and I destroyed them. Love, to me, was a mixture of hate, anger, rage, control, and sex. When God called me back to New Mexico, I gave it all up. I gave up men, sex, and relationships so He could heal me. However, my mind was still a battlefield, and I was losing. Lust destroys relationships. Sure, I convinced myself it was okay because I didn't watch porn and I no longer masturbated, so who was I hurting? I was hurting me.

It was a rough morning the day I went for a very serious talk with a family member for healing. I prayed. God laid out the time and wrote the words. I had several people praying for me, and I knew God was involved. I woke up, and all I could think about was sex. What?! I had not thought about my ex-boyfriend in years, and suddenly, everything we did was a playback like a reel from a movie. I then thought about someone else but pretended it happened after we were married, so it was okay, right? *Wrong*. I was so confused. I was so ashamed.

I asked God, "What is going on here?!" He said, *"You are trying to run from pain. You think you can stop thinking about how this person hurt you if you think about other stuff."* You can't run from the pain; it is always there until you deal with it. Every time I thought about sex, I would lose focus on God and His promises. I would feel horrible. So why did my mind keep going there? Because humans will do anything to escape pain. My mind was trying to not think about the hurt, pain, and trauma, so it thought about something else more pleasant. However, lust is no one's friend. It kills, steals, and destroys. Lust doesn't stop at just movie reels in your mind. It steals everything. It steals your peace, your relationships, and your healing. There is no gray area here. Lust is a counterfeit of love. It is not okay to just have bad thought patterns or turn on that computer. Lust is lust, and it will destroy everything in its path. It will make you a slave and take away your peace. It may be fun temporarily, but it will always end up destroying you.

God told me I had to choose. I can't have lust and God. I might get hit with a lustful thought that I had no control over, but I could control every thought after. If I could stop the thoughts after the first one, I would win the battle in my mind. Every time I chose lust, I agreed with the enemy's plan for my life. I was running from God to escape the pain. If I kept agreeing with the enemy, I was never going to have healing and always be stuck. God designed sex for marriage between two people who trust each other and who share everything in life together. It is to bring honor, respect, and an extension of God's love to the person you are with. It is not for physical selfish release or for escape from pain. It is not designed to harm or disrespect the other person. Lust takes everything God intended for sex to be and twists it into something it is not intended to be. If you are taking part in sex based on lust and not God's original design, it isn't expressing God's original design. If you have sex because you need to recover from a bad day or are trying to escape your painful marriage, then you are sinning. Lust cannot fix your marriage or help you with a difficult day. Anything that becomes an idol is a sin. So yes, sex can be a sin, even in marriage.

I concluded that if I wanted healing, I had to invite God in now and let Him restore me. I had to choose to stop thinking about sex to escape the pain. I had to agree with God's original design for me and let Him restore me and my thoughts. It was hard at first. It was like someone pounding on the wall of my brain to get in. I just kept thinking, *I will not agree with the enemy's plan for my life. To give in is to kick God out and let the enemy destroy me. I will not think about sex to give me a few minutes of relief from a lifetime of pain.* I have experienced freedom like never before, and there is less and less pounding on the wall of my brain. I am free to understand and experience real love now. I am free from shame and guilt. I am renewed in His purity. I am innocent once again.

I want to talk to you about restoration, forgiveness, and moving forward in Jesus's name. This process has been a unique journey. I felt irrational most days, but God always came through. I don't know why I had to do what I did, but God does. All I can tell you is a very broken woman has been transformed into one completely healed in Jesus's name. I had to kick out my pain demon, have God rewire my brain, pray, step out in faith, ask for forgiveness, be honest with my parents, and, the biggest thing of all, believe. I wrote a poem about believing. Then, God spent the next few days changing my point of reference. It is all coming together.

Without belief, you cannot have a relationship with God. If you have a back door or a backup plan, then you don't truly believe in God. I am going to be honest. I confess I have thought what if or maybe the whole journey. Despite this, God has given me several signs that I am hearing correctly, and I have not believed Him. I have had a "maybe" or even "if" attitude the whole time. The truth is, I thought, *What if I believed God 100 percent and He disappointed me? What if He does not come through? Then that means even He disappoints. Even He hurts, and even He doesn't love me*. God has been very clear that my disbelief was a problem, and I needed to let go of doubt and unbelief. I need to believe Him 100 percent, or I don't have a real relationship with Him. I won't be able to trust Him or have faith unless I believe what He says is true. I can't keep having escape plans. I am either all in or all out. It has been very difficult to be so vulnerable with God and choose to believe Him completely. That is faith and where God is. This whole walk is about faith, trust, love, and belief in the Trinity.

God told me that I could choose to stay in my past and keep digging up the pain, *or* I could choose His restored future for me. He promised me my childhood, my marriage, and my children would all be restored and that there was no wasted time. The biggest gift that I have is choice. God will love me no matter what I choose. That is called unconditional love. So here I am, crying my eyes out, amazed at God because even now, He is working something out for my good. I can see my healing and restoration, as well as the restorative healing of my family and friends. All I had to do was surrender to God's perfect plan, step out in faith, believe, and choose.

The choice has always been yours. Your past can be forgiven, redeemed, and restored. You just need to choose. Will you continue to walk in your past and be a slave, or will you choose to know you are a child of God? You are forgiven, and you are restored. Either way, God loves you. He has unconditional love for you. Either way, He will continue to guide you and take care of you. He does not love you any less or more because of your choices.

I leave you with this: I finally got to a place where I was tired of the enemy lying to me. He does not play fair. He attacked me at a young age, and I thought he robbed me of many years of my life. But God is the God of Restoration, and He restored my youth and my life. I finally know who I am. I am the daughter of a King. I will not be shaken. I will take up the authority given to me and fight. With God as my leader, I will always win.

The enemy cannot steal what God has given you. Aren't you tired? Aren't you tired of losing to the enemy? Aren't you tired of being held prisoner by lust, brokenness, suicidal thoughts, self-pity, and the false identity of the victim? I sure was. I encourage you to go on the journey God has for you. You will win. You will be healed. You will be a conqueror in Christ. Fight, my fellow kings and queens. Fight, my fellow God-ordained warriors. No weapon formed against you shall prosper. Stand in the gap for your loved ones. Fight! The enemy is a *liar*. He is not a friend. His promises only offer death. God gave me life in just one breath. Breathe it in, put on your full armor of God, and fight. Your life is not over. God has a special purpose for you. You will win!

WINNING THE BATTLE THROUGH MOURNING

I sit here, and I reflect. I mourn because my life feels like a counterfeit.

The lies I believed stole so many years from me. I wonder if the wounds that stole my innocence can possibly ever compare to the wounds You endured for my transgressions. The love that I believed, and thought was real, is that the same love that convicted You with a death sentence?

Now I realize that the counterfeit love I believed in was not unconditional. It always carried a cost. One You were willing to pay just for me. For Your love has no conditions, it is free. I wonder if the lies they used to convict You were the same lies I believed were true. The prince of lies who told the crowd to turn on You was the same liar who made me run from You.

The shame I felt and the guilt I endured, is that the same feeling Pilate felt as he sentenced You to death? Did he really have a choice? I feel so much pain and sensitivity as You break all these generational curses off me. How can that even compare to each smack of the whip that cut You and tore Your flesh?

As You are healing me and I cry in pain, have I forgotten the price You paid for me? When I complain about being weary, I can't imagine how You felt on that walk. Full of blood, sweat, and tears, and carrying a cross. When I cry out how unfair this is, how can that weigh up to sentencing an innocent man? A death. You paid for a sin you never committed, but I was guilty. As they hammered the nails into Your hands, was that for each angry word I spewed? As they placed the nail into Your feet, was that for every lie I bought into? Was that crown of thorns placed on Your head for all the times I wish I was dead?

I was acting out in my false identity of anger, rage, pain, and hate. Can't You see I was broken at such a young age? As I sit here and mourn all that I have lost, did I ever count the cost? The one You paid on that cross. While You hung there in so much pain, I know You already knew my name. I know that I was on Your mind as You felt the pain and agony.

You whispered, *"Forgive them, for they know not what they do."* Jesus, did You say that directly to me? Broken beyond repair and believing lies destroyed my life. But You saw my heart and chose to die for what I really was deep inside.

Was it me that knelt under that cross, where You humbly counted the cost? Each drop of blood covered all my sins. Each burden you bore just to restore. When You died, I fell with despair. Jesus, did You really leave me here? Please tell me hope does not put me to shame. Why did You go away? For three days, I suffered with all my doubts. *Does He really keep His promises? Can I believe what He says is true?* Jesus, where are You?

As You went to hell to take back the keys of death and returned to my heart to unlock the door, I was lying on the floor begging You to take my life. All my hope was gone, and I had nothing left. But You breathed life back into me as You took Your first breath.

The same Jesus that died and rose again came and restored my brokenness. He resurrected my once counterfeit life and made me whole again. He entered my heart, and by His stripes, I was healed.

I may mourn for the night, but joy comes in the morning because Jesus fought for my glory. Jesus, I don't deserve Your sacrifice, but You came just to save my life. Why would You want to save me? What can I give You in return? You give me everything. So here is my life, Lord, I freely offer to You. For if Your love was so great You died for me, then I must learn to love me too.

No more lies or counterfeits. I choose to live with joy instead. You sacrificed everything. You used my mourning to open my eyes. The truth is in the One who gave me life. Better now to see the lies than fade away the rest of time. You fought for me and kicked out the enemy, for You are the Prince of Peace.

You are the champion of a hard-fought battle for my beautiful soul. And I thank You forever more.

STEP INTO THE LIGHT

"It's been several months now since You have exposed my past. Carefully maneuvering through the traffic of all my self-inflicted wounds, You pulled out every piece of my trauma, baggage, and brokenness. You wanted me to embrace the dark.

"The person who I am is no longer a slave. You exposed it so I could step into the light. I needed to see and to be saved, and only You could do it. You rewired my brain and removed all the demonic influences in my life. You showed me all the lies."

You said, "Embrace the past that hunts you. You don't belong in that place anymore. I always had a different path for you. My daughter, don't you see your future is positioned in victory? I have done all the work for you. Now all that is left is you must choose. No one else can make your choice. You can dig up more from your past, and I will always let you hear My loving voice. But, daughter, I release you into so much more joy.

"Walk in the new life I have set for you. You don't have to do anything but follow My narrow path. I will thrust you onward and guide you. Let go, My daughter, and let Me lead. I created places for you as I interceded.

"No longer a slave but My masterpiece. Let Me love you the way I always intended to. Don't ignore the dark, but don't stay there either. My daughter, won't you choose the path I have for you? Will you believe I have provided for your good? My name is Love, and that is what I am and do. My daughter, you are free to run and breathe. Trust Me, and choose your new life of light as you break through."

DO YOU BELIEVE?

"Do you believe I love you?"
"Yes, Lord, I believe, and I love You."

"Do you believe I have only good for you?"
"Yes, Lord, I believe and thank You."

"Do you believe I have a future laid out for you in victory?"
"Yes, Lord, I believe I am standing in Your victory."

"Do you believe I know how to lead?"
"Yes, Lord, I believe, and please lead me."

"Do you believe I can be trusted?"
"Yes, Lord, I believe, and I completely trust You."

"Do you believe I can restore all that was stolen from you?"
"Yes, Lord, I believe I am new in You."

"Do you believe I can give back your childhood?"
"If you say so; yes, Lord, I believe."

"Do you believe I can restore your innocence and purity?"
"Yes, Lord, I believe; I am pure in You."

"Do you believe I am healing you back to your original design?"
"Yes, Lord, and thank You. You do it in Your own time."

"Do you believe My timing is good,
even if it is not your timing?"
"Yes, Lord, Your will is set and perfect for me."

"Do you believe in My promise for marriage and children I have
given just for you?"
"Yes, Lord, I believe, and I breathlessly await."

"Do you believe in a fairy tale I made just for you?"
"Yes, Lord, I believe You are my fairy tale, and You have so
much more in store for me."

"Do you believe you know who I am?"
"Yes, Lord, I believe, and You reveal so much
more to me every day."

"Do you believe all My promises will come true?"
"Yes, Lord, I believe, but help my unbelief."

"Do you believe you're completely forgiven and
deserving of My forgiveness?"
"Yes, Lord, I believe. Thank You for the cross
and the blood You shed for me."

"Rachael, do you really believe in Me? Because without belief
and knowing who I am, you can never be everything I designed
you to be. You are so important to Me. Without faith, hope, and
love, you will never really know who I am. But, My daughter, you
must believe Me and know My character. Then, you will stand on
unshakable ground. I am your rock. I will protect you."

"God, I do believe You are everything You say I am. I trust that
You will lead me and guide me in Your will. You are all I need

and nothing more. God, all I have is my belief in You, and that is enough. Thank You for patiently waiting for me to believe. Thank You for pursuing me."

DRAW NEAR TO ME

"My daughter, won't you draw near? I feel like you are always going over there. I want you here by My side. Won't you just sit down and rest?

"My daughter, I have you. I promise I won't let you go. I see your heart and all your fears. I promise I did not put them there. Stop trying to be perfect; that is not My demand. I just want you to understand who I am—a Father who loves you—but you keep hiding.

"Where are you? I know you want to be everything I designed you to be, so why won't you come find Me? I never left you; I am always by your side. Won't you come and let Me help you survive?

"I need you to rest; come lie down by Me. I promise, My daughter, I will meet all your needs. I simply just need you to believe. Yes, I have you and I will lead. Yes, I love you more than anything. Yes, I see your heart's desire, but first, come sit by this fire. I made it just for you. Come and sit here and know Me completely.

"Know that I am good and pure. Know that I can only love you. My daughter, it was not Me who stole your childhood. It was not Me who hurt you. I am here to restore you. I love you, and I always will. My daughter, come draw near to Me. I want to heal you completely."

BEAUTY IN THE CHOICE

I truly believe the power of God is in the choice He gives us. I can choose to believe the lies the enemy tells me, or I can believe in the power of Christ.

Every time I entertain a lie, my life becomes a battlefield. Dodging death, destruction, and counterfeits, I feel my hopes become despair, as I believe the enemy will always be there. Waging war on my soul, telling me I have no hope. I will never be anything more than whatever lie I choose to believe.

But in my pain and in my flesh, God whispers His truth into my ear,

> *"O My daughter, won't you choose to hear Me correctly? Choose Me because I am hope. My words are life and full of joy. You are so much more than you think you are. The enemy is just the father of lies. You are not what he says you are. You just must choose My heart. I will give it freely to you. It has no room for the lies you have been told. When the enemy comes around, you must choose not to entertain his silly game. What he offers won't set you free, for it will keep you in captivity.*
>
> *"Choose to believe what I say is true. Even when*

it does not look like it is so. You don't have to understand; you just need to know who I am. I will always fight for you. I will never fail you. I am good, and I have a plan. It will all work out better than you could imagine.

"Choose to go against your flesh. The offer of its freedom is temporary; it only really offers death. It will be hard to follow My narrow path, but it leads to never-ending happiness.

"Choose to not let the enemy in, no matter how tempting his promises are. Choose to know who I am. Freedom is letting go. I will take all your burdens from you. Won't you come to Me and rest? I have already fought the battle for you. Won't you just believe what I say is true? I will win, and I will make everything perfect for you.

"All you must do is choose."

THE END OF A JOURNEY

I sit here, and I contemplate the end of a journey that lasted for decades.

I was living behind self-created bars. Living behind a door locked shut to hide all my doubts. Shame invaded my whole being, but on the outside, I smiled pleasantly. I had to conceal what was going on inside of me.

You came along and flung the door open. You sent me an invitation to join You in a life full of freedom. No longer a slave because my debt has been paid. All I must do is choose the ransom You paid in full.

But the waves are crashing around me, and I am tempted to run back to a shelter of my own creation, which offers no hope.

I have finally decided to understand that You are my rock, the firm foundation on which I stand.

Although my circumstances try to convince me it is my last chance, I see You are the canopy within which I hide while You fight for me. A promise You made and won't take away. The gift You give is in the choice I make. My eyes deceive me into seeing the fairy tale of Your promise as my worst nightmare. *Did he really leave? Don't I deserve to be pursued and not left instead?*

Or can I believe hope will not put me to shame and understand the story has not ended yet, for You do not create lies and counterfeits? Your promise is only to show Your glory.

My choices are to believe in You or the enemy. Do I take each thought captive and bring it to Your will? Or do I let it run away with temporary pain relief and a continued lifetime of slavery?

The enemy can only steal, kill, and destroy. You can only love, restore, and resurrect all the dreams I have ever known.

For the first time, I started to dream again. A childhood activity restored, which was always robbed from me. It is beautiful to believe that my life was made for more than death. I will believe all You say about my life is true. I dare to dream and wait on You.

Waiting on Your timing has healed my broken soul. O, how I have come to love the journey I had to take. For healing is in Your name. I will never forget this time with You. The pain You helped guide me through. How You held my hand and were always close. You never left my side.

You owe me nothing, but still give me everything. So, I will delight in my heart's desire, believing Romans 8:28 is completely true. I am excited as I expect the beautiful revealing of Your unique story for my life.

God, I choose You.

LIFE IS IN THE WATER

I have decided to lift a heavy weight. This weight has haunted me for so long that I could not breathe, a past that threatened to take life from me. You always had a better plan in store.

As I declare that You will always have first place, I can't wait to let the water of Your life come flowing through my veins. I step into the water and prepare as You start lifting all my despair. When I walk closer to take that plunge, I feel hope start to invade the darkness that has lived in my soul for too long.

God, as You put Your hands over my mouth and nose to dip me into Your life forevermore, I think of how I could not breathe, but You breathed Your life into me. As my lungs cried out for air, You were there to breathe Your resurrected life into me.

As the water starts to come over me, I finally realize I am free. I feel every chain breaking off me. I come up from that water, and I feel the rush of Your life releasing liberty. Now I see. I am free. His new life has just washed over me. I declare to the world, I *believe*. For I am new and no longer in captivity.

I am forgiven of all my sins. I walk away believing all of God's promises. My past doesn't haunt or define me anymore. No matter what was buried in that wound. God has pulled and destroyed its claim for my soul.

Freedom is in His name. That water is like His blood, it washed away my sin and doubt. I choose to believe I am new and walk in a future laid out in victory.

My God has raised life and dreams back inside of me. Since I am His child, I laugh uncontrollably. For He has returned my innocence, and now I am clean. O, how I am so glad I made this choice. For don't you see? Life is in the water my God gives to me.

WAS IT WORTH
THE PAIN I ENDURED?

As I look back, I ponder if the countless months full of pain and rage were worth the price I had to pay. I started off being so angry with You. Dare I say that You were the target of all my rage? I screamed, and I yelled. I said the worst things I have ever said. I did not respect, nor did I trust. God, I wondered how this could be for my good.

I was in a fantasy land. I was trying to pretend I was what I said I was, but I was a liar and a counterfeit who was boldly proclaiming Your name.

Yet behind closed doors, I didn't even know who You proclaim You are. So, I lie on my floor, and I throw my fists, banging them in a fit of rage. I swear someone probably would have thought I was acting like I was two years old. I was just screaming at You, "How could You?" and "Why, God, do You lie? Why did You pull up my counterfeit life?"

But at that moment, covered in misery, I looked at You and said, "If we are going to remove it, then remove it all. I don't want anything that's counterfeit left." So, You took away every single lie as I had to relive every reason why I didn't trust You at all, the shame, the abuse, and all that rage.

O God, could this all really be worth the wait? Couldn't You have just protected me at such a young age? All that anger made me hate men. It kept me from thinking You were good. I believed it was You who had wasted ten years of my sacrifice, waiting, praying, and keeping myself pure.

A promise You gave, but there is no end in sight. For he just walked away. God, did I just waste my life? Did I not hear You correctly or do it just right? Did I not pray and ask others to pray with me? Did we all hear You incorrectly?

It turns out I was standing on sinking sand, as I contemplated how to run away from Your good plan. I wanted to turn from You and run back to my counterfeits, just to make it all feel good again. But it turns out Your love for me, and me for You, would not let me leave. I felt like You took everything. Now I see You were just changing me.

Then, suddenly, I lost hope. God, they say that You are good, but this doesn't feel right. They say You will use it, and it will be worth it in the end. But all I feel is pain and death. That night, I thought to myself, *Maybe it's time to end my life.* I felt like everything in me was gone, but one thing kept holding on.

God, You came to me, and You whispered hope. In that hope, I decided to trust. All thanks to You, I am still alive. You broke through with all Your truth. Your light and life destroyed the enemy. You broke my chains, and hope became light.

For the first time, my eyes were open; all I could see was the love You have for me. You brought me closer to Your heart and revealed Your true Self. Now, I know You better than ever before. You did not have to take all my abuse. You saw my heart and knew I was worth the pursuit.

God of glory and wonder, how beautiful You are to me. You restored all that was broken and changed my lies back to Your truth. You breathe Your grace and blessings over me. You said I was worth the fight, and now I am free. I was once so broken and full of lies, but You put me back together by Your grace and love. I am so full of gratitude for You saved me from my own demise.

Was it all worth it in the end? God, I would go through this experience a million more times to know You like I know You now.

Thank You, God, for calling me Your own. You are worth everything.

A MOTHER'S HEART

A mother's heart is so complex.

Full of wonder and bewilderment.

From the time her child takes their first breath,

Her heart begins to beat with new excitement.

For nothing compares to a mother's love.

It's full of grace and innocence.

It's pure and a reflection of God's own heart.

Her job is to bring God's love into us.

Nothing is as pure as a mother's hug.

It's full of life, warmth, and love.

There is nothing in life more desired than that kind of touch.

When I fell and scraped my knee,

You were the one who comforted me.

You kissed me and told me it would be okay.

I always knew you would be there for me.

My memories of you reading countless stories to me just before
bed, I cherish up to this day.

You were there for my first heartbreak.

You told me it would be okay.

You are the one who taught me how to pray.

All the years I ran away,

You fought for me at the Father's throne.

It is you I can thank for every good trait that I own.

You make me laugh and taught me how to have fun.

Your advice always leads me to God's heart.

Even when I hurt you,

Your arms are always open to take me back.

I know you are my home.

Thank you, Mom, for your love, joy, peace, and grace.

I love you more with each passing day.

SUICIDAL THOUGHTS THAT PLAY AROUND IN MY HEAD

Suicidal thoughts play around in my head. Why do you always come around right before I go to bed? You torment and inflict suffering. O, you really do hate me. How did you get back in? Wasn't it God Himself who kicked you out? But here you are again, trying to disguise yourself as an old friend.

You offer control and freedom, but it's an offer you cannot give. Let's be honest and real: how can I have control when I am dead? What freedom comes from a grave? What offer can you really make? You say you want to stop my pain as you are putting me in chains. You're a liar and a counterfeit; your offer only ends in death.

But you know how to play this game, for you have me drowning in all my shame. Who can I tell about these thoughts running around in my brain? I am trapped as you beat me down. No one is around to help me tame these thoughts. For who could understand this kind of pain?

I must keep quiet, for I do not want to offend. I don't know anyone who can handle these thoughts with grace. Will anyone be able to run this race? So, to myself I must keep while you continue to hurt me. Any hope I had, you sucked from me. For you make me believe hope is a dying cause.

Wait, I must stop and think, for there is One who can carry this thought running around in me. His name is Jesus, and He is grace. He urges me to take these thoughts captive and turn them around. Wasn't it Jesus Himself who paid the price? He can offer the debt that I owe.

When you try to run your game, I will think of His frame, for it hung on a cross to kill your name. No longer will I entertain your plan. You are no match to escape the suffering. He paid for my agony with His instead. He calls me daughter and gives me love. I no longer have room for all my self-hate. God's love poured in and offered the best escape.

It is true, and it offers life. I must be so much more than you say I am. Why are you tormenting me anyway? I must have a purpose and a plan that scares you more with each breath that I take. Listen, you must go away. The only jail is around my soul, which is there to keep you out.

There is no longer a vacancy sign hanging on my heart. Now, it is occupied by Christ's love—the love He so freely gives. For just as hard as you fought against me, He lovingly pursued me. So, no more entertaining you. I am too busy immersed in His love, and now I love myself too.

So that means goodbye to you.

UNCONDITIONAL LOVE

Unconditional love is a very confusing concept. Can it really be a tangible thing we can accept? A love that is given without conditions. A love that died for me and offers no contrition. I have loved for so long in all my shame and all my guilt. But for some reason, all my relationships are like flowers that wilt.

As I demand my own way, I only find love that seems to push me further away. As I hear You call me to Your heart, I feel the need to protect myself, and I start to dart. Why would I need to protect myself from the One who died for me? Why is this control and manipulation making me want to flee?

I want to do things on my own. Then blame You for feeling alone. In my pain and all my doubts, I hear You ask me a question quietly because You never shout, *"My daughter, do you love Me unconditionally?"* I know in my heart that the love I give is conditional. If You don't do this or that, then it is done, and my love grows flat. I demand You do things in my time. Or I am convinced You are committing a crime. Then I start to protect myself and make You the bad guy. I think of all the ways I can say goodbye. I start to run and flee, but You keep coming after me.

God, I want to be like Noah, Abraham, and Elijah. But not if You ask me to surrender because then I start acting more like Delilah, creating more harm and someone's downfall.

God, how can I be more like Paul? Trusting You 100 percent and going to jail because of it? Never questioning or blaming You? I just want to be new. The answer seems to be in their love. For they always are looking above.

God, please help me know that kind of love. You say I can if I accept it freely. O God, I want to know You deeply. Yes, God, I want to love You without conditions. Please place me in that position. I no longer want to have suspicions. I just want to be in submission. I want to love without inhibitions. I accept Your proposition and love You without conditions.

Knowing the suffering that I face puts me in a higher position. For Your love always draws me closer to Your heart. God, please help me to restart for I never want to be apart.

I always want to grow closer to Your heart.

PRICELESS

God, I just heard someone say that You see me as priceless. But my heart says that advice is worthless. God, if this is true, then why have so many people put a price tag on me?

If I am priceless, then why did my dad's love come at the price of rage? He loved me just fine until I messed up his plan, and then suddenly, there was a price tag on me. Tell me, who will pay that price for me?

If I am priceless, then why did my mom's love come at a price? For if I did not meet her co-dependency, she also put a price tag on me.

How about the time I tried to protect my brother, and I was five? His friend was twice my size. He threw me up against a wall and strangled me until I could hardly breathe. What price tag was put on me then?

That guy who chased me in the streets. He did not even know me, but I could feel he wanted to put an end to me. What price was I worth to him then?

How about the time I went out with my boyfriend? His friend decided to take away my choice. The shame I had when I could not stop him. He did it in front of all my friends. What price tag did I have, then?

How about the time I loved until I had nothing left? But he cheated on me. Do You think he counted the cost or just put another price on me instead?

I know part of this was my fault. For that, I will take the blame, but God, what about what happened to me at such a young age? I mean, God, do You really wonder why I hate men?

Then, let's talk about Your promise. Didn't I pray just right and do what You said? But he put the lowest price tag on me yet. To go work on a project was that all I cost? Did I just waste my life? Waiting on a debt to be paid.

But didn't he say that he was waiting for me to heal? Wouldn't that price tag be priceless? So, which tag do I believe? Does it really matter? Only One can pay the price. God, You sent Your Son to pay the debt. He took all the price tags off me when He chose to die for me.

How can I repay that kind of debt? Still, He came and loved me. With every horrible event, God still was there protecting me. He saw my heart and held me close. Why would the God of the universe choose me? Why did He choose to heal me? As I yelled and demanded, You came down and answered all my questions. You never left, and You came close.

You orchestrated all of this. What a beautiful story You have told. You continue to write each loving and beautiful event. My life is Yours, and I must see. You tore all the price tags off me.

You call me daughter, and You tell me I am free. I declare that I am priceless.

WHY DO YOU LOVE ME?

"God, You told me to be honest with You, and You would be honest with me. To tell You the truth, I am so tired of hiding. Here is my heart that bleeds as I pour out these fears that lie deep inside of me. God, why do You love me? I feel like such a mess trying to die to my flesh. One day, I am feeling blessed and know exactly who You say I am. Then the next, I am lost, still trying to count the cost that You have already paid.

"But sometimes, I still hate this process. It feels like it will never end. All I ever wanted was to be loved. All You do is offer love unconditional. So why do You feel so far away? I know it wasn't You who pulled away. So why do You love me? A broken mess and a hypocrite. Feeling like I am on a roller coaster. One day, I know exactly who You are. The next, I am ready to run away.

"I really do love You. So why am I so afraid of letting go? I want to be so close to You. I want to unlock my heart and let You in. I want to let You accept me for who I am. But then again, once more, I am trying to be perfect, so I don't need You.

"I know this really isn't true. I want to be so vulnerable with You. My fears and my doubts keep kicking You out. I am so used to protecting myself. I keep asking what if even You hurt me? I know that can't be true because that is not what You do. My insecurities still scream so loud.

"God, I want to be so near to You. Why do You love me when I still blame You and live in all my doubts? The noisy voice of my fears keeps me choosing to numb my heart. I want to let You in, but do You promise not to let me down? All I have ever wanted was to embrace You. To let You hold me as You wipe away all my tears while You continue to tell me You will never waste what You hold dear.

"God, I still feel like I hate men, but You say that means I hate You, too. You made men, and they are in Your image. Even if they have hurt me beyond my limits, I choose to forgive.

"God, I don't want to fight any longer. I have searched, and I have asked. I counted the cost, and I ran away. My heart still longs for You. Can You break in? All I have ever wanted was to be loved. Did I look in all the wrong places?

"God, are You enough? Can You please come fix this broken mess? Can You erase a childhood full of distress, memories that haunt me? Can You heal broken love that always leaves? I am feeling worthless and can hardly breathe. As all my shame and guilt suffocate me, God, will You rescue me? You tell me You will never leave. I can feel You here next to me. Asking me to let You in. Asking me to accept Your love for it is unconditional.

"I try to love with Your love but even with my best intentions, I still come in over aggressive. My heart was in the right place, but I am still such a mess. I want to help restore childlike innocence for all those who have lost it. It has been stolen from so many. But do I try too hard? I am just trying to love all the children. To show them that they are loved and need protection, so their innocence and hope are restored.

"Aren't we all supposed to be Your children? But I don't have one to call my own. God, my deepest desire is being ignored. Why don't You restore the promise You gave? I have been waiting. Still, no one to call me their wife. No child's voice to call me Mommy. Am I not good enough for their love? God, that is why I am going through all of this, to be the best for them.

"Is it fair that You choose me to break all the family curses off my line? Yes, it's an answer to my prayers, but I keep fighting reluctantly. So why do You love me? When You give me all that I ask, I am still dragging my feet. Even when I see You take good care of me. Okay, God, I said my piece. So here You go, I'm giving You the key. You don't have to break in; I give You all of me. Do I really deserve Your love? Can You show me why You give so freely from above?"

> *"My princess and My love, don't you see how loved you are? I paid the price because I wanted you. You are worth all My love. I counted the cost, and you are worth every penny of my affection.*

> *"Don't you see I have always known your perfection? I created you in your mother's womb. I was there, and I never left. I always wanted to be near you.*

> *"My daughter, won't you come here? You're the one that has left. I never counted you as just a guest. My kingdom is still right here. I have a crown waiting for you. Please run in My gardens again. I see you dressed in white with flowers in your hair. You run and laugh with-*

out a care, for you are free here. I am protecting you with My guards. You have a new name. No more guilt or shame. Here, you are royalty. Please come back and take your place next to Me.

"I have thrown a banquet just for you. Come sit here next to Me. Let's laugh and talk about things while you get to know Me again. My daughter, don't you see. I made this fairy tale just for you. Come here; come laugh and play. You are so beautiful, just like I made you. As childlike as I created you, I made you strong and brave, too. You love this kingdom you share with Me. It is right for you to want to fight with Me to help protect the children. Just remember to always fight with My armor.

"You are loved, and you have honor. I made you to be the perfect princess. You will always win if you wait for Me. Don't take on fights I did not call you to. My daughter, don't you see, you will never lose when you fight by My side.

"Come back, My daughter, to a perfect kingdom I made just for you. Can't you see I love you? No need to question, no need to ask. I will always be here. You just have to choose. Come back, My daughter. I am calling out to you. I love you, and I am waiting for you. I always will, and I always have.

"My daughter, I love you."

HOW DO I ACCEPT YOUR LOVE?

God, I cry out to You. I don't know how to get out of this place, but I really want to. I want to draw near to You, but my heart feels so closed off once again.

I know that You are perfect, and You are love. Why do I keep choosing to feel so unloved? I know the problem isn't You. You are asking me to step out in faith. Your promises are great. So why do I want to flee? I feel like I react because of PTSD. Each time I remember their abuse, I keep thinking that it was You. I know that isn't true, but I can't seem to break through.

You keep asking me to do things I don't want to do. Each time, it triggers memories of the abuse. So, how do I let You in? How do I stop fighting? I know there is just one area I won't let You into, but I sure want to. I need You to meet me in this place. Please hold my hand while You walk with me and fill this place with Your grace.

So lost without You. You are everything that my heart requires. Please, God, meet me at the fire that You made just for me. I want to sit down and embrace You. Please tell me You will keep me safe. All I ever wanted was to know Your grace. Tell me that You won't leave me in this place, so hopeless and full of rage. I just want to know that You are safe.

Please lead me out of this place, for it is full of scars. I don't want to run from the dark. My heart is racing so hard. Can You come quiet me? Can You help me not to flee? Can I invite You into this place?

Come take my heart and show me how to accept Your love.

GOD, WHO ARE YOU?

God, I must ask. I really want to know who You are.

My flesh is weak. One minute, I am so sure and excited; the next, I am down and giving up again. My emotions are in a state of disarray. Sometimes, I think that I hear You so distinctly. But when I am proved wrong, I feel like quitting it all.

Dying to my flesh is tough. I just want to know who You are. Every time You get to this place in my heart, the one with all the scars, I fall apart. Where is my love for You when I still question who You are?

Sometimes, I feel like I am trapped, and my escape plans are all shattered. Following Your plan is no easy task. God, are You abusing me? Can't You see these wounds are so deep? I can't move; this is too confusing.

Why do You love me? I am such a mess. Sometimes I hate my flesh. Can't I just be who You made me to be? Why am I still battling all these insecurities? Stepping out in faith without seeing the cost makes me want to give up. God, why am I so weak? The waves keep crashing over me. I really need to know who You are. My heart longs for Your embrace. God, please come meet me in this place.

God, is this who You are? You walked with me and fixed my heart. You held my hand through all my pain. You never left me in the dark, slowly guiding me even when I wanted to flee. You are patient, and You are waiting on me.

I know You never give up on me. Even when I shouted at You, You held me close and said, "I love you." You saw my brokenness and decided to come in and fix me. Even in my doubt, You came in and cleaned me out. You fought for me and died for me. Then You talked to me and walked with me.

For seven months, I was up and down. You just kept hanging around. You comforted me when I would cry. You confronted all my lies. I still don't know what will happen. But God, I know that You will always be by my side. I know that You are not the bad guy. You have always been there for me. So, let me bow down to my knees.

God, I must stop fighting You. You are God, and I am not. Why do I question You? So please accept my apology. God of wonder, God of life, You are a good Counselor, Friend, and Father. I am lucky to be Your bride.

You are powerful and majestic and full of life. So please accept my heart and keep it safe. God of my life, don't let me question You again, for my answer should always be *yes and amen.*

WHEN I WAS FIVE

Dear God, come help me. Once again, I am feeling downcast. How did this get back in? Didn't I just get done saying I love You? Here I sit still, feeling this wound. I still feel like I am being abused. Why did no one help me when I was five? How could they not see it was the year I no longer cried? Shouldn't I have cried when I was dying inside? No one answered. I was just denied. There was no one by my side. I just sat quietly as she put her hands all over me. I had no way out; I was confused, and my choice was taken away.

Even when I confided about these things, they thought it was just innocent. No one stopped her, even when I was not a willing participant. But it's okay. We have never talked about that place. I guess it hid and never revealed its face. Not until it was too late. Then, that guy thought it was fine to throw me against a wall. Don't worry, I didn't even shout. For heaven's sake, he was twice my size. My dad came to save me, but he was full of rage. Guess what we never talked about that day?

Then, shortly after, I got sent to that place. She watched us but treated us like yesterday's waste. In fact, when I asked for chocolate cereal, she let her kids feed me dirt instead. They laughed and pointed, but I didn't cry. Who would dry my eyes? It was not until I came home with a full set of bite marks my parents said sayonara and goodbye.

Plus, let's not count all the surgeries. They asked my mom what was wrong with me. They did not mention how they argued and grabbed me in a sensitive location. I was scared as they yelled at each other. Then, I didn't wake up for several hours. I was sick and so scared that they would not send me home. They kept asking my mom, "Why doesn't she cry?"

God, all this happened when I was five. It taught me not to cry. I decided I had to fight. I learned not to let anyone inside. That's why I thought it was strange when You asked me to let him in. You said to let him be the leader, and then all the trauma started again. He became the enemy every time he tried to break inside of me.

A heart guarded for so long. A concept that was way long gone. It scares me to invite anyone behind these walls. I can't do it. I won't. Don't You see? No one helps you when you cry. God, even You became the bad guy. I don't like anyone to lead because they always leave.

All I really wanted was someone to hold my hand, walk with me, and show their love. So why did I always choose to do it alone? I wanted to leave and throw it all away, but You kept pushing me to stay. You had to take me back to this place and meet me here. You never give up. You always chase. You had me go at a quick pace, for You longed for my embrace. God, meet me in this place. I can't do it alone. I need You on Your throne.

A lot can happen when you are five. It can make you thrive or make you wither up inside. A child's innocence should be protected. But since it wasn't, please give me a new perspective. God, meet me in this place. Grab my face and wipe away these tears. I choose now to freely give to You. It's time I leave behind these scars and meet You, for You never harm. You just want me to feel alive. Can You undo what was done when I was five?

AGAPE LOVE

"My daughter, I Agape you."

"O God, I love You. You're just like a friend to me. Yes, I have a few doubts, but You are my favorite thing. I tell people about You, and I make big claims. But please don't ask me to do too much in Your name. That would be scary, and I really don't want to be put to shame. I mean, do You really expect me to proclaim anything that isn't tame? What if You don't show up? Wouldn't that be quite lame? I don't want to make false claims. So, I will just keep my faith small and make sure You fit in my box.

"Yes, God, I Phileo You."

"My daughter, I Agape you."

"You have asked me again. Perhaps I missed something in the first campaign. I want to get to know You more. So, let me explore. Who are You, God? Can it be You are more than what I have been proclaiming? Did I perhaps put You in a box? Aren't You asking me to act a little bit unorthodox? Okay, this is scary, but I will let You accept this burden I carry. I will spend more time with You. Getting to know what You say is true. Wow, God, I see now that there is more than just proclaiming Your name. I want to bring more notice to Your frame. Is what the Bible says about You true? I still have certain issues, like why this situation does not make sense. Why is my situation and everyone still in suspense? Are

You good, and do You keep Your promises? Can I trust You 100 percent? I don't know, God. My faith is growing, but sometimes, You still feel absent. I still wonder if this pain will ever end.

"Yes, God, I Phileo You."

"My daughter, I Agape you."

"Okay, this is the third time You have said this. What has gone amiss? I don't want to be like Peter because he seemed to pay no attention to the matter. Let's see, God, I have counted all my cost. With You, nothing has been lost.

"You have changed me. I no longer want to flee. You have brought me through so many things, like all my pain and counterfeits. You have been so passionate. I keep expecting You to hurt me, but You keep doing the opposite. I admit, I forgive all men. I have lived through my trauma, and I have forgiven.

"You ask me to step out in faith. Okay, I will take that bait. For I fully trust You. I must make a choice. The choice is You, no matter what. You don't lie, and You keep Your promises.

"Okay, God, I am all in. I surrender all to You. You have made me new. RIP to the old me, for she is dead and gone forevermore. God, I will take this adventure with You. I choose to love You unconditionally.

"Yes, God, I Agape You."

WAITING

God, I am waiting to hear from You. I want to try something new, so here I wait. I dare not move. I am waiting for You to carefully approve.

I tried running from You. But nothing good happened when I withdrew. God, here I wait. I want to hear from You. Let's face it: this was way overdue.

I have my hands lifted out, and I am on my knees. So here is my heart, Lord, do with it as You please. Here I wait, God, I wait patiently. Honestly, I am sick and tired of my complacency. Meet me here, God, for I want to know You more. I don't want You to be the God I made before.

Please reveal Your true nature to me. That is the only way I will be free. God, come and embrace me. At last, I have come to agree. Let me bow down to my knees, God, as I wait patiently.

GIVING UP CONTROL

Giving up control is hard to do, but I think it is time to see life from a different point of view.

What would life be like without my logic? That kind of thinking has become chronic.

Does it make sense, or can I see it? If not, then heck no, I am not going to submit. I want to control the way my life goes. If not, I feel like You are trying to impose. Control has no room for faith. To which will my heart lay claim?

Control, are you really an old friend? Have you really been a companion to me? Because you don't match the things I decree.

Dear God, have my life and my heart too. O wait, that's not comfortable, and I don't like that now, so I am running away from You.

I keep making God the enemy. But wasn't it my control that caused me to flee? I am starting to feel all my anxiety. Every time God tries to break down the walls inside of me. I keep trying to find a little control. Building a wall up around my heart has become my goal.

Sure God, I will obey You. But I will not let You through. This wall is so strong, I can't let Your love in. But I am really dying within. O God, how do I let go? Because I really do want to know.

But what if I do and You don't come through? Can You really make me new? God, are You safe? Will You protect me? God, please help; I want to be free. But I keep fighting You.

I am so scared to try something new. What if I jump and You don't catch me? What if I give You the key? Will You save me? I just want a guarantee. But is that faith? Just in case, will You promise if I surrender my control? Will You soothe me and guard my soul?

Control, you are suffocating me. I no longer want to agree. I feel so miserable. This control is making me so irritable. It has stolen all my joy. It only comes to destroy. Control is really a decoy. Pretending to give you something you enjoy. But it's really keeping you from God's heart.

I never want to be apart. So, God this is really challenging to do. Help me surrender this control to You.

DEAR DAD

Dear Dad,

I love you.

Sometimes, I think you don't feel like this statement is true. But I promise you, there is no one I admire more than you.

I still remember being young and dancing in the living room. Dancing to the Monkeys took away all my gloom.

I can't wait for you to meet my groom. I can't wait for you to walk me down the aisle so afterward, we can dance to the Monkeys with style, just like we used to; this thought makes me smile.

I can't wait until my children see you in the same light. As a grandpa, you will feel like someone new. You will be so great at it because you always pursue.

Things were not always perfect. But I love this time God has given us to reconnect, and I want you to know I see you with respect.

I know you are hurting and feeling a wound. But God is where those answers will be found. So let Him be your solid ground.

Dad, I love you with a love that is so brand new. No more wounds or counterfeits, for this love is true.

THE EMBRACE OF MY DAD

Dear God,

I come to You. For right now I need you to fill a great wound. Please, God, I am asking You for a different view. My heart is heavy, and I must confess that right now, I need You.

Please show me this situation from Your heart's view. Separate what is false from what is true.

I loved my dad, and I miss him so dearly. So please answer this question clearly.

Are You embracing and taking good care of my daddy? Because right now, I hurt so badly. Yet when I close my eyes, I can see You near. God, I know that You are right here.

I see my dad up there with You. I can see him embracing You and becoming new. No more pain and no more fear. He is laughing because You are here.

I can see my dad smile, and I can see him run. Look, God, he is having so much fun!

God, he doesn't seem to have a care at all. In this place here with You, I can recall. All the moments he held my hand, he helped me to understand.

Life wasn't always an easy journey, but with my dad standing by my side, there was nothing to concern me.

When I think of him, I smile from within. I remember his roots run deep as they flow inside of me, for I am a product of his tree.

Who he was, I am still. When I cry and my heart hurts, let these memories refill, for I am a part of his legacy that will be passed on to my family.

God, when my heart starts to hurt, and I can take no more, please come into my heart and restore. Help me to remember his face. Let me see You as both of us feel your embrace.

(This poem was written for a dear friend who lost her dad.)

REVEALING MY FATHER
ON FATHER'S DAY

God, I am weary. Please come sit near to me.

See, I did it again. I fought You as I screamed, dying within. I keep getting mad at You. I really do need a different view. I keep thinking You come to abuse.

God, I've kept getting stuck in the same situation. I'm still trying manipulation. God, I am angry with You. So right now, my heart, I choose to withdraw. I keep thinking You're making me into a fool, which makes me think that You are cruel.

God, what are You doing? Shouldn't he be the one who is pursuing? Seems I am stuck in a cycle of insanity. This feels like inhumanity. Are You good? Are You safe? God, do You love me? Is there some guarantee?

God, my emotions are suffocating me. Are You saying I must agree? God, this does not make sense. I didn't choose for them to take my innocence. I realize I am still living like a victim. I need this out of my system.

God, cure the source and not just the symptom. My heart is so closed off to you. Even though I know how hard You pursue. It happened when I was five. You know that is when true love was deprived.

So, You keep trying to come after me. I keep trying to flee. As of today, it has been three weeks in a row. I keep being obedient and then screaming no! I keep having thoughts of suicide. And still, You keep saying You're the one who died. You did it just for me so I could live knowing I am free.

So, instead of repeating the situation, let me make You my foundation. I just took Communion and invited You to change my perspective. I know that revealing Your heart to me is Your main objective.

You're not the bad guy I made You to be. You just want me to be free. You love me and want to know me fully. You want to give me Your promise, but first, I must stop treating you like you're a bully. So today, I choose to stop fighting You. Instead, I choose to let Your real character come through. No more living just to die.

I choose You to show me how to live and be my supply. Thank You for doing this on Father's Day. Revealing Your character as my Abba Father today.

IN LIMBO

As I sit here in limbo, I am giving You a very small window. I am starting to grow cold. I just want a simple yes or no. I feel trapped, and I can't move. I keep waiting for this situation to improve. But God, I feel like I'm stuck in insanity. I get mad at You and start screaming profanity. I don't want to, but somehow, I keep coming unglued.

Oh God, where are You? You keep saying You are right here. You tell me to have no fear. I keep choosing pain instead of love. I keep trying to look anywhere except above. You say that You will restore it better than it ever was before.

A child, You have just for me if I would simply stop and no longer flee. You say that You will restore what has been lost. But it came at a big cost. I see the hope You have put in me. The tears I have cried have watered that seed.

Finally, now, I am starting to feel free. God, can it be? I feel this hope inside of this broken soul. In this moment, I want to give up my control. As I sit here in complete dependency, I can see that You're asking me to surrender my old tendency.

For three weeks, You put me on repeat. And I kept trying to retreat. But on the third attempt, I tried something new. I finally decided to listen to You.

Feels like I met You for the first time on Father's Day. I finally decided it was time to obey. I no longer see You as the abuser I made You to be. I can see You as the God who paid a great price for my guarantee.

Then suddenly, all my fears and anxieties tried to break in. But You had already started to change me from within. There is a lot placed on a father's shoulders. The one I placed on Yours was as big as a boulder. Don't worry, God, I know that You can handle it.

Instead, you wrote me a fairy tale and asked me to submit. You asked me to get rid of all my old *friends*. Those demons had to come to their end. You asked me to go through the mourning that won the battle for my broken soul, for it was in Your blood that my heart would be consoled. I had to embrace the dark before I could step into the light. That is where You showed me how to fight. You asked me to believe. You just wanted me to know You would never leave.

Then You called to me, saying,

> *"My daughter, won't you draw near? This limbo is hard if you don't ask Me to be here. But beauty is in the choice. Don't you see I gave you a voice? My daughter, let this be the end of this journey. Won't you let your heart come and return to Me? For life is in the water. Come home, My daughter. I promise you it was worth the pain in the end. I know you needed Me to be a good friend. A mother's heart is what you need. So please, daughter, let go of those suicidal thoughts that play around in your head, for they only mislead. With them, you must learn to disagree. They are blocking My unconditional*

love.

"Don't you see you are priceless? That is what I say from above. You ask why do I love you. Because I am your Bridegroom. I see you dressed in white. I know you have put up a good fight. You keep asking Me how to accept My love. My daughter, just give it to the beloved. You keep asking me, 'God, who are You?' But every time I answer, you keep coming unglued. Be still, My daughter, don't you see? I know what was done when you were five. But I want more from you than to simply just survive. Agape love is what I am calling you to. My daughter, it is time to be renewed. Can you please wait here patiently? My daughter, please stop treating Me so ungraciously. It's time to give up your control. It is time for Me to make you whole. Can you please address Me as your dear Dad? I promise you I am not bad. It is time to meet your heavenly Father, as I am revealing myself on Father's Day. Come over here and embrace your Dad."

Today is the day I see what this limbo is for. My God wanted to end the war. I felt trapped in my situation. I kept trying to use logical information. I must have read thirty books trying to increase my knowledge. But this isn't college. I needed a real love experience with You. That is why I always came unglued. Who would want to go through all this pain? For there was nothing that remained. I fought You repeatedly. God, I just really hated men. I never knew that included You. So, You had to accompany me through. I couldn't do this on my own. I need You on Your throne.

In my weakness, I need You to be strong. This is what You wanted all along, to surrender my dependency. There was not a way out if I continued to try to do it independently. So, as I fought my depression and asked You to come in, You met me there, and for the first time, I won. That broken five-year-old who was crying out to You, she met her King today. You came through. I lay on that floor, crying with joy and relief because I could finally enjoy the release.

God, for seven months, I was up and down. In one minute, You turned my whole life around. I just needed to surrender to You. I needed to experience that state of limbo, for that was the only way I would let You grab hold of me. I needed to be dependent on You 100 percent. God, that is how You removed my dissent.

GOODBYE TO THE FIVE-YEAR-OLD WITHIN

Today, I say goodbye to you. For today, I will become something new.

I thought limbo was the end of my story. It turns out, there is more I must do for God's glory. This is what the whole adventure was for because I had never seen you before.

You're a liar and a counterfeit. I just never really had a true encounter. You have tried to kill me for so many years. You have caused me so many tears. You're no friend to me. With you, I could never be free.

I was five, and I was scared. You came to me and acted like you cared. You promised you would protect me. That point of view made me want to flee. You told me that God wasn't safe. You told me how I needed to behave. You said, "Don't let anybody in," but you always caused me to sin.

You screamed at me that God didn't love me, which caused me to choose the wrong key. I opened doors that I should have never walked through. You tried to convince me God could not pursue. I had to stop agreeing with you. For what you said was never true. I screamed, I yelled, and I tried to kill myself. All the while, you disguised yourself. Saying you would protect me. Yeah, right, you just did not want to let me be free.

You pushed me to the brink of insanity. This almost cost me my spirituality. How could God be what you say? I thought I was to obey. But something was not adding up, for I felt like I was corrupt. Every time I did what He said, I became undone. And yet, this must mean that your work has just begun.

You keep screaming to grab the gun. I don't understand why I can't listen to God. I feel like my whole life is a facade. Claiming to love God and following Him. He asked me to jump in and swim. I just sank, but it wasn't Him who did not catch me. It was you who led me out to sea—then left me there to drown.

However, there were too many people around. They saw you not as a five-year-old. No, you are a demon I let take control. I can't agree with you anymore. I need God to restore. I can see that He is trustworthy. When it comes to my heart, He is more than worthy.

So, goodbye to the demon who acts like she is five. Because with you, I will not survive. I know God will protect me. It's a guarantee. He will fight my battles. He is the only thing that matters. He always wins.

So, let this new life begin. I no longer agree with you. It's time I withdrew. I am going to run to my Father. So don't even bother. You know how this ends. We are not friends.

God always comes for what is His. He always does what He says. You do nothing but destroy. You are just a decoy. God is everything He promises, and He is a good friend. To my five-year-old demon enemy, your contract with me has come to an end.

I sign my life over to the One who gave me His. For that is where my freedom begins.

UNITY

Unity is a word we say a lot in church, but do we really practice it?

Before this journey, I felt like we were all just split. Hiding away in my pain. Letting thoughts run around wildly in my brain. I did not want to become undone. So, I just pretended and started to run.

I don't want to feel shame. What if I reached out and no one came? My fears and my anxieties started to overtake me. I started to feel like I would never be free. Until one day, I could take no more. I felt like my life was a war. I reached out, and you all came. I have never been the same.

A demon I agreed with for thirty years. She is the one that caused all my tears. She tried to kill me several times. She tried to commit various crimes with all of you standing by my side. I could no longer hide behind my pride.

I am so thankful for you all. Without you, I would have never climbed past that wall. I am alive because you spoke the truth. For I was still stuck in all the lies I had believed from my youth. I thought playing with my life was just a game. When I saw how scared and how upset that made you, I was never the same.

My life matters, and it comes at a cost. Let's face it: these issues I am facing are not soft. But I know that without all my friends who stood with me, my life would have been lost. You prayed for me and drew closer to the Lord. This was your and my reward.

This situation was not an easy one. Unfortunately, it had to be done. I know God is growing you, too. I can see how He is making all of you new. Thank you for helping me. For now, we are all three. This cord is not easily broken.

So, I hope this never goes unspoken. I love you, and I want you to know when it's your turn, please come to me. That way, I can pray for you and wait for God to speak, for that is the key.

Unity is about involving God, too, so we can see things through His point of view. It will not always make sense. But you don't have to be on the defense. I am not judging you. I am listening to see what God says is true. That is true unity. Listening to God as a community.

FAITH

Faith is acting like it is so, even when it is not so.

However, the completion of this promise seems to be slow. I asked eight months ago if You could grow my faith. I did not realize it would take so many days. I have been up and down and all around, for it took a while to expose this wound. I feel like I am irrational, and having faith feels crazy. It is not for the lazy.

I have prayed, read, and asked to find You. There were days I did not think I would make it through. You dared me to have dreams and asked me to have hope. After months of doing this, I had to learn how to cope. When things don't go my way, I must realize that things don't always happen today.

You are still in control. You are fighting for my soul. Not having faith, dreams, and hopes means I don't know You at all. What I wanted was so small. I wanted marriage, kids, and a white picket fence. You wanted me to stop fighting Your plan and acting out in self-defense.

I realize I have never really known You. I have always looked at life from my point of view. Opening doors before Your time. That way, in my opinion, You could commit no crime. Because making a choice before You could answer in faith allowed me to choose my own way.

For if I walk in faith and you don't come through, would I be okay? God, is that what You do? Don't You always come through? So why am I doubting You? I know You just want to make me new.

So, I have done crazy things. I started to imagine beautiful rings that we would both wear. But without him here, my heart started to despair. There are things in my closet I made for my wedding. Except I think he is forgetting. I don't know if he remembers who I am. Or if he is even listening to the one true Lamb.

God, You are not the God who would give me false dreams, even if things don't appear like they seem. I have fought You and been stuck in insanity. I just need to stop agreeing with a lie and feeling like You would cause calamity.

I have prophecy of the kids You have for me. And I hear You say there will be three. I have seen my house, and You say the foundation is good. God, is it possible I have misunderstood? Did You dare me to dream just to put me to shame?

I did this all to proclaim. I thought I was honoring You. Are all these dreams and hopes true? I keep asking You. You keep coming through. But what do I do when it hasn't yet come true?

You never forget the One who paid the debt. So please don't let me get upset. I want to have passionate faith and believe in You until it all comes true.

GOD KEEPS HIS PROMISES

God always keeps His promises. He does not need accomplices.

I have tried to help Him the whole way, for this situation seems to be gray. God, my promise just said he didn't want me. Is it time for me to flee? I am so confused; I stepped out in faith and did exactly what You said to do. Are You not going to come through? It happened after I wrote "In Limbo." Did You really do all this to make me look like a bimbo?

God, this doesn't make sense. Did I just let the five-year-old back in? You keep telling me to believe and to have faith, but there is such a war within. So, I ask myself a complex but simple question: God, are You enough?

This situation is getting so rough. Will I still love a God who doesn't keep His promises? But that can't be who You are; at least, that is what my mama says. So, did I hear You wrong? I have been doing this for so long. Thirty years, I've asked You, why should I want to live? How can You expect me to forget and forgive? Especially with everything that happened to me when I was five. I have just been fighting to stay alive.

You asked me, "Why? Don't you know who I am?
Don't you know I am the sacrificial Lamb? Why
would you think I would lie? Haven't I replied?

You set out your fleeces. I've always answered you, but you always fall into pieces.

"Miracles are not what you need. You just need to trust Me to lead. My daughter, I have moved mountains and have shown My glory. Haven't I written this whole story? You know that I don't lie. I just need to be your entire supply. Do you trust Me or think I am safe? If so, why do you keep acting like you are unsafe? I love you, can't you see? So, My daughter, can't you just agree? I need you to stop losing faith and to believe. Things are not how you perceive.

"I have control of this situation. Stop trying to use knowledge and information. Don't you know I already know what is about to happen? I know both of your passions. I know both of your wounds. I know both of your moods. None of this is out of My control. I am just working on his and your souls.

"I can change hearts whenever I please. Let Me do this, for this is My expertise. You want to get rid of the five-year-old? Then let go and let it all unfold. Your next assignment is to just wait patiently. And to look at Me graciously. My daughter, won't you just let go? I will fight this battle for you without a woe. Who do you say I am? Am I enough for you as a sacrificial Lamb?"

God, You are safe, and I trust You. I know You have made me new. I love You, and I know You love me. I am finally free. I believe You are doing something in this beautiful, unique story. It is all to shine Your glory. Everyone involved is changing and seeing You in it. So, I think it is time that I submit. The only way to kick her out is to believe what You say is true. God, I know You will come through. No matter what I finally see, You are all I need, for You are my only guarantee. Yes, God, You are enough for me.

GOODNESS

I keep trying to see how this is good. Because from my point of view, it seems that You must have misunderstood. God, this is not what I asked for. To be honest, I was too busy trying to keep the score. Is it me, or is it him who didn't do what You said?

God, You are asking me to wait patiently, for this dream isn't dead. You keep telling me to humble myself and break down my pride. It is time for me to come to You and abide. As I sat there and questioned You, I realized that the only thing that is good in me is You; that is what is true.

If left up to my own devices, I would have gone to all my old vices. Let's be honest, I would be dead. How about I just choose You instead? I renewed my vows with You the other day. Here, I am questioning You again today. God, I know You are good. So, I asked You to reveal Yourself to me because I knew You would.

You keep asking me to get excited. I know this is a gift You offer to me, and I should be delighted. I just have never had this feeling before. I am a little afraid to explore. A few times, I've tried to have hope and excitement. It just felt like an assignment. I tried to let my soul explore this feeling. It never seemed all that appealing, for it has always disappointed me. It has no guarantees.

God, what can I do when I know You are good, but I keep feeling mistrust in You? I see that You always pursue. I just can't center my thoughts on You. I need a different view. For now, I will just keep choosing You.

Your goodness is the only thing that will see me through. I am tired and ready to throw in the towel. I can't make that inner vow. Here I am, relying on You. Your goodness always comes through. I am nothing without the goodness You put in me. His name is the Holy Spirit, and He is always striving to set me free.

No matter what I think or feel is right, You are the only thing that gives me delight. Dear God, I choose the goodness that You offer me. I will let You set me free.

BOLDNESS

I am sorry, God; it seems I have forgotten. I have been continuing with caution. That is not who You made me to be. My authority comes from the Trinity.

I stand at the right hand of Your throne, for I am not alone. You sit right next to me.

Finally, I am free.

I boldly claim what You say is true. Because You always come through. People may say that I am crazy. That is because my mission is no longer hazy. I have tested You, and You have shown me that all I see is from You.

I will no longer become unglued. My identity has always been to be Your child. You say You love me as You smile. You cast out all the demons I was agreeing with. What they told me were a bunch of myths.

You showed me all my counterfeits. For that life was found unfit. That's no way for a daughter of a King to live. You always wanted me to do so much more than just survive. You want me to thrive. God, You say, *"Stand up and claim My name. This will bring Me fame.*

> *"My glory is all there is to this story. You will no longer keep inventory. Who cares how many*

days it takes? For I do not make mistakes. Stop comparing who I am treating better. I am not a forgetter. I will do all that I promise, and I will not delay. Stop demanding your own way. Now, stop hiding and feeling shame. It is time to make these bold claims, for the promise did not come from you. I always come through.

"Stand up and shout to the world, 'My God does what He says He will.' He is a God who fulfills. No more hesitating. Stop relying on your limited information. It is time for My children to see they have authority. Do not act like the majority. Step out in faith and boldly proclaim because you will never be the same.

"My children, don't you see? You are so much more than what you are living. So, will you stop being so unforgiving? Just step out and love without fear of rejection. I alone will be your protection. First, you must step out of your bondage. You are no longer a hostage.

"You are My child, and I love you. So boldly proclaim all I say is true."

I SAVED THIS DANCE FOR YOU

Dear God,

I needed You. Today, You really came through. I was stuck in all my doubts, for I had been in a long drought. I feel Your presence and meet You for a little while. But this has been a tough trial.

I started doubting You again. All You wanted me to do was say yes and amen. Why is it so hard to believe? Is it in the way I perceive? So, I asked You to meet me in this place, for I was showing You very little grace. I turned on my worship music and asked You to come join me. See, I could not hear You in all the noise from the demons with which I chose to agree.

I did not want to wait patiently. I wanted to live complacently. God, that is not who You are. You came to heal my scars. I closed my eyes, and You were there. You held my hands and told me that You saw it wasn't fair.

You apologized in place of all the ones who were supposed to love me but shamed me instead. You apologized for everything they said. You told me that You never intended that for me. Then You told me You were not like those men. You spoke Your love over me with such intensity. Then You said, "This is Your true identity. A daughter of a King."

Then suddenly, my cold winter heart melted into spring. I saw myself dressed in white, with flowers on my dress. I was no longer in distress. I laughed uncontrollably as joy washed over me. For what seemed like an eternity, I was dancing with the Three. You spun me around and waltzed with me. You showed me how to truly be free.

You walked me by still waters on the most beautiful mountain. Your love was pouring over me like a fountain. You said You would take care of me. You said Your promise was a guarantee. I just need to wait patiently. You said to make sure to come back to this place more than occasionally. O God, I will never forget my time dancing with You. That is the day You made me new.

You filled me with excitement, hope, and dreams. With You by my side, nothing is as bad as it seems. I decided to be a better bride. I had to let go of all my pride. I decided to renew my vows and have a real wedding day. You led me into our vows and showed me how to pray. God, You asked me if I would save a dance for You.

Yes, God, for dancing with You is where my dreams come true.

BREAKING GENERATIONAL CURSES

The biggest lie I ever believed is a lie that I made up. That I am who I am, and that's corrupt. A statement I told myself, "That's how I grew up," is what defined my personality. However, it is God who defines me in all actuality.

I had been praying for over a year for God to break generational curses from me. I thought it was just for me to be free. But what it would truly mean, I did not see. This process would be painful and take so much time. And encourage me to write all these rhymes.

God had a different plan: to help not just me but all the families involved, for this is the only way things can truly get resolved.

No more alcoholism, rage, and co-dependency. I will no longer function out of my emotions, control, or my old tendency. I choose to live in God, functioning on complete dependency. Where I am weak, He is strong. To Him, I belong.

I was trying to live out of my pain and control. It was killing my soul. I prayed, and God answered me. However, the way He did it made me want to flee. I needed to break these curses off me. It was the only way to be free. I would have done things in my own way. It would have led my children astray. How could I protect them when I was too busy pulling away? Trying to make them pay a debt that wasn't theirs to pay. I acted out in anger, suicide, self-harm, and demanding things my own way. These actions would not be okay.

My mom has been praying for all these years. Little did she know it was to make up for all my tears. I know they did their best, and they helped me to grow. They introduced me to God, and that brought the overflow. They owe me nothing, and they are the ones who began to break this curse. Now, it's time to shut down the enemy by taking this curse and doing the reverse. Through God and this journey, I proclaim all the generational curses die with me. That way, my children will be free.

GOD IS ENOUGH

"I have been asking myself why. Why did I let a whole year go by? You told me to get excited. To act like we were in step and united. Instead, I treated him like the enemy, for pain was my only identity.

"So, You did what You had to do. You pulled him so You could pursue. I was so angry at You. I didn't think You would come through. I wasted all this time trying to convince myself You committed a big crime. I wanted to blame You and walk away. I want to do everything my own way.

"People kept asking me if You were enough for me. I always answered no and talked about how I wanted to flee. See I couldn't understand how You were good. I felt very much misunderstood.

"The truth is You wanted me to do this without pain. I kept agreeing with the demons who were screaming inside of my brain. They tortured me and screamed how You were not good. They tried to hurt me and kill me as often as they could.

"So, for a whole year, I fought You. I went back to what's familiar, and I started to want to withdraw. I just did not understand Your big plan. That is when all the traumas began. It wasn't You who hurt me.

"When You heal wounds, it doesn't harm but sets me free. I kept agreeing with the demons instead. They kept screaming that

You mislead. Control, irrationality, pain, suicide, harm, and a demon who claimed to protect me. It all consumed me.

"They would not let me be. So, You patiently exposed every one of them until nothing was left. For the first time, I could feel my heart beating inside my chest. I asked You to reveal Your true character to me. You came to me and said, *'Hello, I am the God who is enough, and I am everything I claim to be.*

'I am enough to take away all this pain. I am enough to help you choose to never agree with those demons again. I am enough to make My promise come without delay. I am enough that you will never feel like you must demand your own way. I am enough that you will see I am good. I am enough that you will never again feel misunderstood. I am enough to restore everything you have lost. I am enough; that is why I died on the cross. I am enough, and I will keep My promise. My daughter, stop being a doubting Thomas.

'I am enough, My daughter, don't you see? All you will ever need is We Three. Am I enough for you when you don't receive that apology you feel like you deserve? I am enough, and I will restore; all you need to do is serve. I will fight your battle for you. I am enough, and I am making you renewed. My daughter, just sit and wait patiently. I am enough, and I will come through more than occasionally. I always win, and I always come through. So, sit and rest, and let Me do what I always do. I make beauty out of ashes. I am about ready to make more than splashes. Get excited and jump with joy. The God who is enough is ready to give you a life you can enjoy.'

"Thank You, God; I can see this is what the whole journey is for. You are enough for me, and You just came and restored."

WEDDING DAY

I decided to meet You today. After almost a year, I decided it was finally time to obey.

I heard You say, *"Put on your wedding dress."* God, I will look like such a mess. Last time I put it on to meet You, I had to cut it off. When I tried it on, it was so tight I couldn't even cough. You told me it was okay. It was time to put away my old ways, for You had another dress You wanted to showcase. Hey, that day was right before this drama all began, right before my whole life was undone. I wrote You such a beautiful letter, saying I wanted to get to know You better. Eight months later, You have completely changed my whole world. I never imagined dancing with You and getting twirled.

So here I stand, God, I look like a disaster. You told me, "Don't worry," You would be our pastor. My dress was cut, unable to zip up, and very old-fashioned. But Trinity looked at me with such passion. My wedding veil wouldn't stay on. But I was still the one You were waiting upon. I don't see what You see. If I were You, I would have let me be.

Instead of flowers in my hand, I held a lantern to light the way. You told me it was to shine Your glory for the rest of my days. I laughed because, God, what kind of bride can I be? Look at me. Definitely, You are out of my league, which is a guarantee. You Three looked at me as You gathered around to hold my hand and said, *"You're perfect."*

In that instant, I knew my heart was safe and You would never neglect. I have been crying out for You all these years. I wanted You to calm all my fears. I was trying so hard to be perfect for You. You never wanted perfect; You just wanted to make me new. Here I stand such a mess in front of You. But do You still want to say I do? What can I offer to You? Why do You always pursue? I heard You say, *"My bride, I just want you."*

For the first time, I knew in my heart that was true. Here I am, God, broken, messy, battered, and bruised. Honestly, at times, I feel confused. One thing I know is all I really want is You. To know You and see life, people, and my circumstances through Your view.

God, look, You have made me new. I know everything You say is true. You're a God who always shows up. You always fill my cup. I am overflowing with all this joy. No more believing in a decoy. I am so excited to spend my life getting to know You. Will You give me a new lens to see You through? Will You reveal something new about Your character every day?

You tell me, *"My bride, you know I will, now let My glory be on display. I love you, and I have committed My whole life to you. So, let's not go back to the past and try to review. Let's move forward, rejoicing and becoming new. It's time to restore your childhood; it's time I watched you grow. My bride, I love you. My love is what is always true."*

What a beautiful wedding it was all along. Because broken messed up me finally found where she belonged.

WHO AM I?

"Who am I, God? I want to know. I think it is time for me to grow. I don't want to be the woman I was before. I want to be the daughter You restore.

"I give You permission to shine Your light on me. I want to be truly free. What kind of person would You like me to be? For it is with Your plan that I want to agree.

"Who am I when I don't have my fears and doubts? Can I really learn to respond without having to shout? Who am I without a past that haunts me? Who am I without the abuse and mistreatment that caused me to want to flee?

"God, I want to see myself with Your perspective. I want to live the beautiful life that You have selected. I don't want to run to my counterfeits. That life I found unfit. I don't want to be the me I was before. I want to agree with the life You have given me that has been restored.

"So, I ask again, who did You make me to be? I want to know who I am when I share my life completely with the Three."

> *"My daughter, you like to laugh, and you like to play. When you look at Me and trust Me completely, you relax, knowing everything will be okay. You like to run and be carefree. You come running and throw your arms around Me; that*

is when I set free.

"You are full of joy, and it overflows to others. That is why someday, you will make such a good mother. You're innocent, and you see the best in people. You hate and fight against evil. You love to dance and to lead everyone around you in the dance, too. You like to show others how to see themselves through My point of view.

"My daughter, you like hugs. My love is your only drug. You spread My love around like it is contagious. My daughter, that is because you are so courageous.

"I made your heart full of wonder and adventure. You enjoy all of this when you are in full surrender. You get excited and can't wait to encourage others to get excited with you. You just want to share and talk about what is true. When you see life through My view, then there isn't anybody you won't pursue.

"There are no wounds or need to protect yourself from others. You must start living from My love that you have uncovered.

"There is no rejection or abuse. Just choose to stay in the love that I constantly produce.

"You are proactive, and you fight for Me. When you fight by My side, so many people become free. You know how to rest, stay still, and be as you wait patiently on Me. Don't you see, My

daughter, this is who I made you to be? This is you when you choose to be free."

HUMILITY

Do I want God to humble me? I don't know because my pride is wanting to disagree.

I like it when I feel right. But this isn't black or white.

If I can say I am better than men, then I don't feel bad for sinning again. However, that does not make me a better person within. I need to see that I am no better than them. So, who am I to condemn?

If I were Eve, I would have grabbed that apple, for I love knowledge even if it puts me in shackles.

I realized God loves us all the same. We all put too many transgressions on that frame. The minute I understood that I was no better than anyone else, the ice around my heart started to melt. I realized we are all the same. Our sins are unique but still to blame.

Now, I see people in a different light and realize I no longer need to fight. So, I told pride it had to flee. Then, suddenly, all my demons started to leave me.

My pride had interfered with the way that I loved. It stole the glory from the Beloved. When my pride tries to come back in, then I start to run to all my sins. It rips me away from my peace, freedom, and purpose. And all my anger, anxiety, and insanity start to surface.

Every day, I wake up, and I ask God, "Please humble me and fill me up." My emotions keep trying to control me, but God keeps filling my cup. So, my decision is to choose You every day, every hour, and every minute. To choose God's love and accept people without limits. We all struggle, and we all have our sin. It's not my place to judge what is going on within. I don't want to carry that burden.

Then, God kept sending me sermons, saying to humble myself and start thinking of myself less. I know God, I have no more pride left. What more do I have left to confess?

> *He said, "Please share this prophecy." Um, no thanks, God, I don't know them or this company's policy. I don't want to look like a fool. God said, "Who are you thinking about more, My child and Me or the rules? My daughter, I have given you a gift. Your pride is the only thing that needs to shift. Come be humble to Me. Stop thinking about yourself and your guarantee. If you are so humble, why don't you let anyone get a word in? Stop talking and listen; that is where being humble begins. Stop demanding your own way. Trust Me, love others, and know it will be okay. Stop thinking about yourself so much. Be confident in the gift I give you, and start showing people how much of their life I can touch. Let go and listen carefully. To be humble, you must approach people and situations prayerfully. Stop trying to protect yourself and prove you're right. Go to your prayer closet and learn how to fight. Be willing to always listen to Me. If*

you're humble, you will not disagree. Even if it isn't fair, just surrender it to Me in prayer. Love without conditions. This is not a competition. If you humble yourself and stand in humility, then you will have tranquility."

TIME

Time is no friend to me. I want time to happen on a guarantee.

God gives me promises and says it's on its way. Thank You, God, but You need to give me the exact day.

I will not wait for months or years. I am tired, can't You see these tears? I demand that the time is now. Waiting patiently is not allowed. I mean, it has been eight months. Well, ten years and eight months if You're counting, and that feels like a bunch.

Stop telling me it is on its way. If that does not mean it is today. Would You tell a child every day You are going to Disneyland? No, the anticipation is more than they could withstand.

So, come on, God, why are You taking so long? This feels so wrong! I am getting angry again. Can't You just tell me when? This obsession with things happening in my own time is suffocating me. It makes me want to flee. I know that I can't demand You keep Your promise. I see that I am acting like a doubting Thomas.

Doing things in my own time has been our family crime. It is our biggest generational curse. I know I must do the reverse.

I just don't know if I can surrender this to You. I know it's the biggest thing left, and it is stopping me from being new. God, it is all I know. Will You help me grow?

I can see how demanding things in my time caused lots of pain.

Demanding my time on all my relationships has been in vain. It has hurt so many people when I don't give them space. It keeps me from giving God, loved ones, or myself any grace.

Why am I holding on to it with such a tight grip? I feel like I am being hit with a whip. My time control is abusing me. It keeps me from being free. I need to let go. I'm beginning to see that I don't really need to know. If You promised and said it will be amazing. Then, in Your promise and You, I need to start praising.

So here we go; this might be the toughest thing I have ever done. Goodbye, my obsession with time, for you must be undone. You have plagued me and my family for so long. I know that you thought that you were strong. God has been undoing you all along. Time is out of my control. Look at how much of my life you stole.

God, I give it back to You. The promise, time, and the battle are all Yours to pursue. I am going to sit here and wait for You. Because I know You make me new.

GOD, MY FATHER

This whole journey I have been wondering one thing. Are You really the King? Are You a good Father? Or just a Dad who can't be bothered? Do You answer Your promises? Can I really live life without my protective harnesses?

You see, I want to make sure I don't do all this only to look like a fool. I am stepping out in faith, for You wouldn't make me an example or a tool.

People keep saying, what if He did all this just so you can be made new? I look at them and ask, "Can this really be the image of God you believe is true? A God who makes a promise and doesn't come through? How would that make me new? What kind of Father do you think He is? A Father who doesn't do what He says?"

It's not like I did all this without a safety net. I laid my fleeces, asked my pastors, and watched miracles get met. I am sorry, I can't agree with you. I think you need a different view. For that is not the Father I know. My Father wants me to grow. Please read this story and come and see, for this is the story that set me free. Yes, I am still waiting on God. At least I am no longer living my life through a facade.

Let me tell you about my Father. Even when I was a mess, angry, and confused, He treated me with honor. He is a Father who always shows up. When I screamed at Him and told Him I had nothing left, He came and filled up my cup. He never grew tired of me asking Him to answer another fleece. He understood that I just needed proof for some peace. When I dared Him by saying, "If this person has any doubt, I am out." Then God had him answer, "This is your husband, I have no doubt."

God did not get angry with me. He just did everything to set me free. He did it with so much love and passion. All I have ever seen is His compassion. Every time I say I am going to leave, God meets me to reveal Himself to me. He shows up every time; it is a guarantee. He held my hands and wiped away my tears. He whispered loving things into my ear to calm all my fears. He sent me friends to walk me through. All the while He was talking to them, He made them new. In fact, everyone in this story grew.

That is the Father I have come to know. Every situation and everything He stirs in me just begins to glow. He showed me lovingly how to set down my pride. He humbled me as He stood there by my side. I started to see a person I never knew. I started to see who I was through His view.

I can't believe He never left me. I don't deserve Him because, for thirty years, it was the demons with whom I agreed. He saw past the worst parts of me. He stood by my side the whole time I cried, and He set my whole heart free. A God with so much patience, I can never understand. Neither could you if you heard all the times I screamed for Him to meet my demand. He knew my plan was not the best for me. So, He kept sending people, books, movies, and sermons to help me finally agree. God, Your plan is so much better than mine.

Here is my life God; it's time I let You design. Please renew my mind. For every thought from the enemy that tells me You won't come through, I want to bind. I choose to believe that it will all come through. Even if right now I can't prove it to be true, for I don't need to see what You are going to do. I just need to know You are the God who always comes through.

What a good father You are, for You have taken me so far. You are a God who loves me, keeps me safe, protects me, and gives me so much grace. My heart comes alive every time I feel Your embrace. All my fears and anxiety melt away every time I see Your face. Your smile gives me joy. Your truth chases away all the counterfeits and decoys. All I have left is You.

Well, that is good because You are all that I am into. People asked me if this journey was worth it. Yes, of course, because I learned You are a good Father to whom I could surrender.

I SURRENDER

"All this time people have told me I need to surrender my promise back to You. Every time I ask if that is what You want me to do, You say that isn't true. You know, if I lay my promises down, I will walk away and never turn around. Letting people go was never hard for me to do; that is why I have so many wounds. You know I have tried to give him back to You more times than we both can count. You keep saying that is not what this whole thing is about.

"You wanted me to see who You are and have a relationship with You. This circumstance was what you used to show me I had a bad view. If I couldn't even trust You to lead, then there was no way I could listen to what he said. What chance did he have, for if I believed You could hurt me; my hope was dead.

"I spent my life running from You. The whole time telling the world and myself You were the One I pursued. The truth is I hadn't surrendered it all. Let's face it: this wasn't small. I didn't really know who You were. Not while I was listening to her.

"That demon was not a friend. She acted like she was going to protect me, but she was just playing pretend. How do I surrender something You say to not let go of? I hear You say,

'My daughter, you treat it with love. Stop trying to control and demand your own way. Just be-

cause I say, it is all on the way does not mean it has to be today.

'Live your life and find out who you are, for you have come so far. Keep asking Me to reveal Myself. Stop trying to put him on the shelf. I want you to pray persistently. Knowing that it will not happen instantly. You need to be patient and wait on Me. My promise still stands, and the timing is still true; this is a guarantee.

'Daughter, laugh and get excited, for it is already on its way. Enjoy the adventure and put your joy on display. Look at all the people that have profited from this journey. Stop coming to Me, acting like an attorney. I know what I said, you don't have to keep reminding Me. Just let go and agree. My daughter, won't you surrender this story back to Me? I will fight this battle and win it for you. All you must do is agree.'

"Yes, God, I will give this story back to You, for I know that You will come through. I will wait patiently. I will continue to pray more than occasionally. I will be persistent but calm. I will be like David was when he wrote the psalms.

"I know that You are my canopy and refuge. I will no longer choose insanity by trying to fight and refuse. I will wait with gratitude. I will give You my praise and a thankful attitude. I am waiting in childlike expectation. I know You are about to heal and change my generation. I can't wait to see what You do. For I know You will blow my mind and make everything new. I am so glad this is no longer my burden to carry.

"Now that I am surrendering it all to You, life does not seem so scary."

RESTORING THE DAMAGED PART OF ME

I thought this story was over. But let's face it, I am not the owner. I thought "I Surrender" was a good poem to end this story. I mean, what a way to show Your glory.

Then, I kept having disturbing dreams. You said You wanted to interpret what they mean. First, I had to come to this place. For my innocence, You want to replace. O, God, I never wanted to go here. I know this is where I need healing the most; You have made that very clear. I trust You to heal and restore and give me a different view. So here we go, God, come and make me new. This is the part where I need to heal. So, please don't make it a big deal. I will stop rhyming so I can get it all out. I need healing; for this, I have no doubt.

It is hard to let go of lust. By the time I knew what it was, I was already addicted. I was five, and I didn't know what was happening. I knew that it was wrong; I just didn't know why. Satan attacked at an age when I couldn't fight. God, I did not understand the things I was being shown. My innocence, being stolen, temporarily took You off my throne. I wish I knew then what I know now. That lust just steals, kills, and destroys. It wasn't my choice. I didn't understand.

I was five when she made that decision. I didn't even understand what masturbation was until I was thirteen. By then, I was a full-blown addict, and it was my coping mechanism. I thought about things a five-year-old should have never thought about. I was ashamed because I couldn't stop.

Now, my mind is a battlefield. I feel like it has taken me to a dark place as this lust sucks the life out of me. God, how can I even know what love is? I have felt like my body has been a playground for all the times they want to mess around. I didn't ask that boy to touch me in that place. He showed me very little grace. He waited until I was too drunk. He didn't care if my boyfriend was right next to us. Was this love? Why do they keep touching me? Why didn't they just let me be?

I didn't ask for all of this. I never processed all these feelings raging inside of me. I forgot what he did. I forgot that is why I tried to end my life. If this is love, then why would I want it? I have been used for all their benefit. Unfortunately, this is what I learned. They will only love me if I feed their need. All these thoughts festered inside of me. So, I became what I thought they wanted me to be. I was consumed in my lust. Love to me felt like something I should distrust. I just wanted to get off.

I just wanted to have a power surge in me because I thought that meant I won. I wanted the upper hand. I was never satisfied. I always felt so empty inside. I just wanted a real love connection. How could that happen when I don't even know who I am? It ate me up and spit me out. I was never satisfied as it dragged me around. I used people, and sometimes it got dangerous. I didn't care if it hurt them. If they said no, I would become undone. I didn't have a choice, so why should you?

My mind is a zoo. Full of thoughts that put me to disgrace.

I thought I could run this race. The truth is I had no idea how to love. For lust isn't love; it is just a facade. I was addicted at such a young age. I tried to get free, but it has made me captive.

The truth is I am mad at You. Why did You not protect me? Why did no one show me what true love was? Why was I never respected? God, can You restore this painful wound? I really want You to, for You ask me to accept Your gift. I can't because I feel like a counterfeit. My lust destroyed everything You tried to give me. I can't live with both; will You save me?

My mind can't think about loving him. All I can see is what our sex life will be like. Do I really want to marry him? Or just stop feeling this pent-up energy. I don't like who I have become. I am too afraid to love. For all I see is the rejection. I just want Your protection.

I keep trying to choose lust instead of love. I feel like it will keep me safe. For what if I really love him and he never loves me back? What if my heart wants him instead? What if I can't just throw him away? What if he never stays? God, will You meet me in this place? I need abundant grace.

I am scared and confused. I really want to give this to You. It has haunted me since I was five. It has eaten me up inside. I have tried to give it up a million times. But my pain keeps inviting it back inside. It's time I expose this and let you deal with it. I forgive the people who used my body for their own benefit. I choose to let You restore it back to the temple You created it to be.

O God, please come restore me.

PERSPECTIVE

God, I really need Your help. I keep having these thoughts, and they are creating wounds that are making me yelp. I just want to see life through Your lens, for my heart needs a good cleanse.

These thoughts are suffocating me, telling me that You will disappoint me, and they beg me to agree. I don't want to think You could hurt me. I want to believe You are doing this to set me free. I keep reading the letters I sent to him. Every time I do, my outlook feels so grim. How could he not see how much I love him and want to only do what is right? My hope always seems to fade at night.

I don't think I am mad at him. It's You I am mad at; will You make me sink or swim? I only did what You asked me to. Shouldn't he be the one to pursue? Did You do this to make me look like a fool? God, this situation feels so cruel.

I am trying to give up my trauma and my abuse. Honestly, I am just looking for an excuse. I keep hearing voices in my head. They say I would be better off dead, that You will never come through, that Your promise isn't true. It seems that my only hope is from a grave. Living like this is making me into a slave. I need to know that I can choose love over pain. I feel like this has all been a campaign. To see what kind of Father You are. Because, right now my promise, the life You showed me, and all my dreams seem so far.

I feel like I can't make it any longer. I really wish I could be much stronger. I really hate mood swings up and down. It makes me feel like a clown. One minute I am on the highest of highs. Then, suddenly, I wanted to say my goodbyes.

I hate fighting with these suicidal thoughts. For I know this isn't the me You bought. God, I know these are not my own. I just really can't stand feeling alone. I want to live life with someone by my side. I am still waiting for the man You say You will provide.

I know this healing was necessary, for this pain was hereditary. But God, does it ever end? Will it ever be the fulfillment of the promise that You will send? God, I am so tired of fighting You. It is Your eyes I need to see this situation through. God, please give me a new perspective, for what I am seeing is based on my feelings, and those are subjective.

> *"O My daughter, don't you see? I am just trying to set you free. You are so much more than you think you are. You are a star. You shine so bright that others see you from afar. This story is to show My glory. You don't need to keep inventory. In the end, you will have so many blessings you won't be able to count.*

> *"The enemy's voice is what you need to discount. Why do you think he is fighting so hard? It makes him sick to see how I hold you in such high regard. He is trying to take you to a grave. By telling you I will always make you a slave. My daughter, that's not what I do. So, whose eyes do you choose to see Me through? You must stop questioning Me. Start telling the enemy you disagree. He knows what your future holds.*

He is trying to take away your goals. He knows that I will use you greatly. It is not just you he is trying to destroy; he hates Me.

"Do you think I won't defend you or My plan? I knew the results of this story before it even began. Hang on, My daughter, I have you in hand. There is no way I won't do what I said I would do. You know that already, too.

"But when you start to feel hope and excitement, you feel so unsteady. You think I am withholding you from being ready. My daughter, you know that isn't true. You know Me deep within, and you know I have overcome sin.

"What version of Me are you choosing to see? How do you perceive us three? Do you see us through a demon's view? Or do you see how I renewed? You already know what to do. My question is, who? Who do you choose to believe? For you will believe whatever version of Me you perceive.

"I will not make this choice for you. I must let you pick which vision you choose to view. My daughter, only one of them brings freedom. Only the true one leads you to My kingdom.

"My daughter, the choice is still yours. Will you choose a perspective of a God who cures? Or will you let the enemy win? He will only lead you back into your sin. Choose My daughter; I will set you free. I am your only guarantee."

WILL YOU PROTECT ME?

It seems I am at it again. I am arguing with my soul and dying from within. I wrote the poem "Restoring the Damaged Part of Me," now I am yelling; I am at a level ten. All I really want is to get to a place where I can say *yes and amen.*

I know the problem isn't You. It is me who believes in things that are not true. How do I stop getting mad at You? The biggest question I am still asking myself is, "Will You protect me?" For I know You do, but the demons I have listened to all these years disagree.

I don't want to be lied to and abused by them anymore. It just seems that when it comes to this area, my heart is a locked door. I want to let You in. But every time I try to let You in, the suicidal thoughts begin. I keep getting mad at You. I guess I always thought a God who allowed this to happen wasn't good and wasn't true. I know this is not the God I know, for You are a God who wants me to grow. At what expense will You heal me? Would You break a promise to set me free? Is that how You protect Your children? For if that is true, won't that cause me to want to still run?

I need to know that You will protect me. God, please give me eyes that see. I am so afraid You are just using this story for Your glory at the expense of making my future gory. I mean, You are God, and You can do what You want. It's Your story, so You can choose to type it out in any font. As Your child, I must be okay with whatever You do. I want to be happy when I say that, but I do not see You through the right view. I can't see how making me go through all this and leaving me alone shows a God who cares, for You are not a God who wastes my tears. I feel like I have lost so many years, living through all my fears.

I think what I fear the most is a God who would use me to prove a point. Seeing You like that would disappoint. I am scared that You will make me take him in any shape. This thought makes me want to escape. Am I supposed to love him if he has been running around? This thought makes me feel bound. Am I supposed to accept him back if he continues to not treat me right? These thoughts make me want to fight.

I just want to know what being Your child looks like. Right now, I feel like going on strike. I read that poem, and I thought about how unfairly I was treated. Then I think of how he left and still hasn't come back, and I get so defeated.

You told me he was safe, so I gave him my heart. I didn't know if that was smart. It is something I have never done before. Now, my heart and mind are at war. God, You told me You would work on him, and it would all be okay. Then he went away. It's been nine months, and I have nothing left. You keep saying to get excited, and You know what is best. I know that I have a choice. You say to choose to rejoice. For it is all on its way, and it will be so great. To me, it feels like a great weight. I know that You want me to give this to You. For this is the way You pursue.

God, will You protect me? For I really want to be free. I have been doubting You in this area my whole life. I have not been a very good wife. So even if I don't understand or know how to, I choose to know You will protect me and make me into the woman You always intended to.

STANDING ON A LEDGE

"Tonight, I will spare You the rhythms. For I really need lots of healing. I am standing on a ledge, wondering what to do next.

"It all happened after I wrote "Restoring the Damaged Part of Me." I have been lowkey angry ever since. See, things have changed, and I no longer come to You with a five-year-old's point of view. I have grown from that place, and I have more grace. As I was talking to You, I heard You say,

> 'My daughter, it is time to jump. You're standing on a ledge, looking down but not committing to My plan. If you stay there, your adrenaline will be too much. There is no rest standing on a ledge. You can't control your breathing, and you can't think about anything else. Standing on a ledge allows you to be in a place where the enemy can beat you up. My daughter, you need to jump.'"

"God, remember the last time when I jumped? I thought You didn't catch me. That is the day I went for the gun. We both know the reason I am still here is because You intervened. It took me ninety days to recover from that place. Yes, it turned out so good. It brought freedom I had never known before. Honestly, God, I don't want to do that again. I realize from that poem, I am still mad at You.

"Can a five-year-old choose lust? Can she say no to its temptation when it was thrown on her and she could not fight? Yet it destroys my whole life. Here I am at thirty-five, just recovering from that blow. Did I deserve that? I didn't know what it was until it was too late. Did I have a choice? How about the five-year-old demon that tore my life apart? Could I have understood what she was doing when I was so young? Did I have a choice? Did You protect me? Did anyone? How could I recognize it was her voice after all these years? I thought her voice was my own. Didn't I kick both out as soon as You showed me how?

"So why am I still in this long drought? Don't I deserve a second chance? Will I be held to judgment because of a five-year-old's poor decision? For sixteen years, You have promised me a husband. For ten years, I have done all You asked me to do. Is this whom You gave me? Is this what I deserve? He left without ever looking back. He didn't even give me a reason. He told me I was his wife, then probably thought, *O wait, we had one fight. I won't answer her for seven months, then I will say, 'You're nice, but my heart knows you're not the one.'*

"Really, God, is this worth eleven years of my life? Do I get a choice, or are You making me pick him? I don't see what You see in him. All I did was show him love for nine months. All he did was show me how unimportant I always was.

"Why God? Why is this my story? You want me to jump. I need to know You will catch me. I need to know that You are good. Right now, I am very mad at You. I don't feel like I deserve all this. I don't feel like I should be punished for the things I did when I was five. Haven't I been punished enough? Why could You not send someone who loves me? Who wants to hold my hand and walk me through? Will anyone ever care about me? Why are You making this so hard? God, what more can I do? I hate that I am so mad at You. I detest that I feel like my life was stolen from me. I despise how I can't just jump and trust You.

"God, will You help me? I don't want to jump and choose to love him. What if he takes years to come back? I don't know if I want to wait that long. Do I get to make any of my own choices? I know You are good and only want good for me. I am sorry, God, I don't see how any of this is good. I just need to see that You keep Your promises. I need to see that You won't hurt me. I need to see that if I jump, You won't use me as an example.

"God, will You ever come through? How do I jump from this ledge? If I turn around and go back and do things in my own way, then I will have lost a year of my life. If I stay here, I will go crazy because there can be no peace. If I jump, will You hurt me? It breaks my heart that I still must ask. God, will I ever believe that You are only good? That all You can do is love me? My experiences tell me differently.

"My life tells me love isn't good. You tell me my perspective is off, that I need to jump so You can show me. God, do I forgive You? Can I let go of all that was stolen from me? Was it my fault when I was five? For that is what I have been hearing my whole life.

"God, if I jump, will You catch me? Will You love me and show me grace? Will You fix this heart that needs to be replaced? Will You show me how to trust and to feel safe? Can I love You? Can I love him? Can I trust the future You want me to dive in? God, I think there is only one thing left to do… I must just jump and trust You."

MY HEART SONG

My heart has been crying out for You my whole life. Tonight, I want to sing my heart song back to You.

You set me free. You waited for me.

I was crying out for You with all these tears. I was stuck in all my fears. I have wanted to meet You for all these years.

In my darkest moment as seen above, I decided to walk away for that jump seemed so far. You came after me. You brought me down to my knees. You hugged me and took all my rage. I was screaming, punching, hitting, and biting as I fought You. I wanted to run away from You. You held me and showered me with love, but You are not the one I wanted to love on. In my anger, I looked at You, and I said, "Why don't You send me someone new?"

A text I got with an invitation that changed my life. Someone decided to sacrifice. As they spoke over me, the rest of the demons started to flee. That unbelief destroyed my life. He wouldn't let go; he was like a vice. Once he was put in his place, I saw You with all Your grace.

My whole life, I knew something was missing between us. It's hard to love You completely when I don't believe the words You say. I decided to meet You night after night. You were always there waiting to embrace. You laugh with me and shower me with joy. I spent my time laughing with You. I don't think I have ever danced with someone as much as I have danced with You.

You sat with me and dried all my tears. You held my hand as I walked through all my fears. You comforted me as I let go of all that abuse. I came to meet with You and pray for him, but it was me You had on Your mind. You shocked my body, and You spoke with authority as You told trauma it had to leave. I felt it gripping so tight I could hardly breathe. But with You speaking truth, it had to flee.

For the first time, I felt my heartbeat. No longer seized by those liars and counterfeits. I finally saw You for who You are. My heart never felt so pure. I was crying because I wanted to meet You all these years. I have worked so hard to try to get You to come near. I have heard Your voice so loud and clear. I just didn't believe You when unbelief whispered in my ear.

Trauma kept trying to pull me back. O God, I don't care because it is no longer there.

Can't You hear my heart sing to You? All I want is to be made new by You. I felt Your love pour into me. It changed me because now I am free. I don't care about anything else. My heart just wants to be where You are.

You poured so much love for him and her into me. All I want is to be the best for you Three. That future looks so beautiful to me. I can hardly wait, but this waiting has transformed me. I know that I can do anything You set before me. I just need to come and sit here with You.

You comfort me and breathe life into me. The enemy can't get to me when I am up here with You. I no longer need to fight. I will rest in Your presence as You hold me tight. I am your friend, daughter, and bride. I just want to spread the love You have shown me tonight. After years of so much hatred, anger, and spite, I just want to surrender this fight. I know who You are, and I have nothing to fear. The enemy has no more authority when I draw near to You. I feel Your joy and love flowing into me.

How can I be mad or prideful with all this light and pureness consuming me? I was living in darkness, but Your light broke through. All I feel is warmth and peace when I am with You. I no longer feel the need to protect myself. For You are King and have all the authority. I know You are watching over me.

I just want to be humbled and lay at Your feet. Time is different here, and I can spend my whole life with You in this place. You look at me and show me so much grace. I hear You say, "My daughter, it's time you go show them who I am. Come back soon. I always want to spend time with you."

My heart is singing a different tune. I don't have to ask what kind of Father You are. It seems my heart has really known all along. It just needs to be rescued from the dark. My heart will always sing for You. You have made me new.

Now, I have survived so much pain. The only thing my heart really wants is Your love flowing through my veins. My heart will sing of Your love, grace, power, peace, and healing embrace. I hope to show the way for those many children who have not yet found their true heart song.

FREEDOM

Today, there is something I must do. Because I know the words God speaks are true.

For so long, I lived my life with unbelief. I was choosing to live in all my grief. One day, out of my brokenness, I decided to start thinking of myself less.

I started to wonder if I really had anything to lose. God's sovereign plan is what I want to choose. I want to stop living out of abuse. I don't want to keep relying on my excuses.

It's not Your fault I choose to sin. You keep fighting for me to win. I keep choosing to blame them. Is it fair for me to condemn? You showed me the wreckage I left behind. And that changed my mind. Tears streamed from my face. I realized I was not giving men or You any grace. How could I judge all these men? For this whole time, I blamed them again and again. The truth is I hurt them just as much as they hurt me. I fell to my knees when I could finally see. It was not about how they hurt me. It was about how I had to humble myself to get set free.

I asked for forgiveness from men I hadn't seen in fifteen years—the ones I blamed for all my tears. God showed me that I was no better than them, for it was my own actions that condemned. I made choices that destroyed these men. I felt my heart break as I remembered every painful sin. How awful I had been.

This asking for forgiveness helped me heal within.

When they started writing back, they started pouring out how they always felt attacked. I realized that they were still hurting from the wounds I left, that the love I offered them was just a theft. I wasn't looking for an apology, for God had to correct my ideology.

I just want to break the chains that were connecting us, for this chronic infection was causing pus. It was time to set all of us free. We all needed to see that we must let this pain go. It has been bringing us so low.

I decided to step out in faith and listen to God. I am not living this life any longer under a facade. I want to be free. Asking for forgiveness and humbling myself was the key. I wanted my heart to reflect the Trinity. I wanted to surrender to His Divinity. So, even if I fall and stumble, I choose to get up and be humble.

I will say sorry more. I will no longer make the Trinity's gifts into a war. I will accept all that They say. For Their truth is the only way.

Freedom is in Their name. In Their truth, my heart lay claim.

WARRIOR

My whole life, I have been told that I am a warrior.

Honestly, I could not be more eager. I have been fighting my own battles my entire life.

I never thought that being a warrior would be how he knew I was his wife.

Instead of fighting in God's glory, I started to try to write my own story. Fighting in my own time and my own way. Forgetting to just trust God and pray. I started to get so weary. In God's plan, I started to become leery.

Until one day, I had nothing left. I became so depressed. I thought I would end my life, for I was looking at God and this story with strife.

Then, God brought me to my knees. He said, *"Will you believe Me, please? I have this story all worked out for you. Start believing what I say is true."*

I began to believe what He said. His love is what I started to want to spread.

I asked Him what it means to be a warrior for His army. He said first, I had to trust He would never harm me. I must wait patiently. He promises His word won't come back vacantly.

I strap on my armor and wait on my bent knee. I see the enemy coming in like a raging sea. I stay still, looking upon God to lead. He says, *"Stay still; continue looking ahead."* I hear the enemy coming in close. My heart beats with anticipation, but it is God who I trust the most. He says, "Continue staying still; your job is to listen and let Me lead."

I feel my heart filling with dread. Why is He letting the enemy get so close? I chose to let His love and grace begin to engross.

I know God always wins, for He is where all my hope begins.

I stay still, and I won't move, for it is my doubt that He wants to remove.

I stay so focused on Him. I will not act on my own whim.

So here I wait to sharpen my sword. For it is His words that help me be restored.

I tighten my belt. For His truth is what I am dealt.

I feel the breastplate that guards my heart. For His righteousness will never depart.

My shoes are dug in as I wait in peace. For His love was the missing piece.

This helmet guards my mind. The enemy I now choose to bind.

Darts are flying at me. I hold up my shield and watch those demons flee.

The enemy is so close now. God shouts, *"Stay bowed. They have no weapons to throw at you. Just remember to see this situation from My view. Hold your tongue and don't agree with them. They are trying to lie to you to cause you to be condemned. Just stay focused on Me. Say yes and amen and agree."*

God, they are right on top of us! He tells me to not worry and *"don't start to fuss. Do you know who I am? I am the sacrificial Lamb."*

I begin to breathe and focus on Him I start to worship and sing His hymns. That is when I see the fight really happens on my knees. I now see the enemy has nothing in their hands. For my inheritance is more than they can withstand.

I finally understand!

They have no power over me. They are the slaves, and I am free. They are already defeated, for the price has already been completed. I did not have to fight this battle, for I am not just cattle. I am His daughter, and He fights for me.

My job as His warrior is just to agree. I see fear in the enemy's eyes, for I am no longer speaking or buying his lies. He shudders in fear when he realizes I am not who I was. I am God's daughter and warrior, and I am fighting for His cause.

God says, *"Get up; it is time to fight."* I turn around and hold up my sword as I claim, "You no longer have a right. I am tearing this contract up that I made with you. For in God, I am made new."

Just like that, the enemy cowers and screams. For I no longer agree with his schemes. He is destroyed. I am overjoyed, for I did not have to fight on my own. I was never alone. God was always sitting on the throne. I just had to see Him there, for He has been answering all my prayers.

Being God's warrior is trusting Him within. I choose now to always let Him win.

BEAUTIFULLY BROKEN

Beautifully broken, I come running after You. For today an old heart You want to make new. No, You don't want to fix or repair. You just want to replace and exchange it from the old one that used to be there.

It wasn't until I admitted how broken I was that You were able to come and fix this mess. You had to pull out all the old memories and emotions I so desperately wanted to repress.

When I just submitted it all to You, You poured Your love in and made me see what was true. I am nothing without You. You are all I need. I just had to trust You to lead.

All these walls You had to break through just to remove this cloud of pain so I could see with a different view. You humbled me until I had nothing to lean on. My old heart had been robbed. The enemy had stolen my identity. Driving me into insanity.

It was in my willingness to pursue You that I had to put my life under review. I wanted to know You as my Dad. Every time I did, I kept expecting something bad.

You had to undo my unbelief. That demon caused me so much grief. I finally chose to feel safe enough with You. That showed me how much I grew.

I cried like I hadn't in years. I mourned the life that wasn't all it appeared. A facade I chose to believe. A life I couldn't achieve. None of that was real.

After ten months, the fake life lost all its appeal. So, I cried, and I let it all go. That is when Your love started to flow.

Abba, Daddy, Pappa, is it true? Are You the Father I never knew? Protective, loving, safe, and pure.

With You, I can now feel secure. I realized I don't need anything more. For my heart, You have just restored.

God, this is Your story. I want to do it all for Your glory.

I am excited with the new life You gave me. I finally feel this burden lifting off, and I am free. I am so desperate for You.

Being dependent on You is what made me new.

God, I want to give my whole life to You. Can I be the broken mess You choose to shine Your image through?

AUTHORITY

Today, I finally found my voice. I realized God has given me a choice.

I am not a slave; I am free. I just must stop my tongue from speaking death and finally agree. I am the daughter God created me to be. I am His daughter, and I know my weapon is my identity.

Yes, I will speak with aggression. I will boldly proclaim Your truth, for I am tired of what the enemy stole from me in my youth. I have heard and believed your lies for so long. I will not listen anymore because knowing my authority has made me strong.

Being a daughter to a King is all I need. My freedom is now guaranteed. So, stop trying to cause me fear. You can't win if I draw near. I am in the throne room next to my Dad. You can't do anything bad. I am free, and you are the slave. You are the one living out of the grave.

I am living in His sweet embrace. For me, He did have to chase. However, when I saw I could step out with authority, I realized I was God's priority. I no longer want to run. I am starting to have so much fun, putting you in your place and showing everyone around me grace. You keep coming at me like you have a weapon. I no longer believe your intimidation, not even for a second. You're a liar and a counterfeit. You can't persuade me because God and I have had a true encounter.

Hear my voice; it roars like the Lion of Judah. Your intimidation and fear are as fake as Buddha. My voice loudly proclaims the truth that God is pouring into my heart. From His presence, I will never want to be apart. When you hear my voice filled with authority, it's you who must come into conformity. You lose all your rights. You can no longer fight. In His throne room, I sit at the right hand of God. Your authority is a facade. You cower in fear. Every time I speak in authority, you must disappear.

To step out in crazy faith, you must know your authority. Don't let the enemy make you feel like a minority. God is good, and He keeps His promises. So don't be like a doubting Thomas. That is where the enemy gets in. If he can distort your identity, then you will start to come undone within. Just step out in faith, use your voice, and trust your Dad. That will make the enemy mad.

I am so tired of seeing what the enemy stole. All these years, you tried to pervert my soul. Well, no more power will I let you have in my life, for it is my authority from God that allows me to no longer live in strife. Listen to my voice because I know I will speak clear. I will say it loud enough so you can hear. It's time for you to disappear. No longer will you have control of my life. I already know I am His wife.

That promise you cannot steal. For I know what God says is real. Get out of here. I will have no fear. You must go when I say. You are not allowed here, so go away.

I am a daughter of the King, and I have had enough of you. What God says about me is the only thing that is true, not my circumstances and the way I feel because feelings are not always real. That's right; I know you see my authority. I know with God being the judge, my verdict of innocent is the majority.

A HEART SET FREE

I am letting these tears fall freely. Because to You, I am trying to give my heart over completely.

You said You were working on him. He came back today, and after ten months, my heart just feels grim. God, I can't see You in the fruit he bears. Is this really the answer to all my prayers? How could You be okay with the sins he throws at me? God, he is not acting like he is free.

So, I come to You angrily, with my guard up. Is this how You want to fill my cup? If this is love, I don't want anything to do with it. If this is what You offer, I no longer want to commit. I will just be Your slave. I will just keep hoping for my grave.

Your daughter and bride, I no longer want to be, for I crave love, which is the missing key. I have sacrificed for so long. How could I have been wrong? God, You tell me Your answer has not changed. He is still my husband, and it has all been arranged.

God, why would I want him? My future looks so dim. I just want to feel Your love. You keep trying to embrace me, and all I can do is shove. I refuse to see things from Your perspective. For myself, I am being so protective. My view of love is so subjective. You came in and started to change things around.

It seems hope is coming out of this wound. What is this new love I have found? Did You just send all my friends to root me on?

Did You just have someone place a small cardinal in my hand to give me an object to put my hope upon?

My heart starts to break for what breaks Yours. This is how I feel secure. Now, my love and hope can endure. I decided to see him from Your point of view. I pray into that vision until it is true.

He is a man of honor. You are getting rid of his pride that causes him dishonor. He will be humble and submitted. This will allow him to be fully committed. I know You will make him into a man who loves.

I see him as innocent and white as a dove. He is funny and kind. He has a pure mind. He walks in honor and victory. His actions will never be contradictory. He will be a pastor and have a healing ministry. God, he will be all about Your industry. He believes only in Your truth. You will return his soul back to his youth. Laughing and making jokes. He will be more than all my hopes.

Therefore, I love him still. I will keep praying and standing in Your will. God, set both of our hearts free. For with Your will, we always want to agree.

LETTING GO

I keep trying to earn Your love. I am trying to make Your story fit like a glove. I do what You say—expecting You to do everything today. When You don't, I lose my hope, causing me to spend all day trying to cope.

I don't think there is a day I don't feel like a failure. So, I spend all my time trying to change my behavior. Why can't I just be? Why can't I just agree? I am so tired of trying to make Your miracle happen. When it doesn't, I feel like packing. I keep trying to move on. I keep asking what I am missing.

God c'mon! You keep urging me to rest. Every time I try to stay still, I get depressed. I need another assignment. This is what makes me feel excited.

Am I asking the wrong question? God, what is my next intervention? What do I need to fix? God, I feel like I am always having conflicts. I beat myself. Are you really supposed to love yourself?

God, just tell me the next thing. I will tell the whole world how You are King. What about another bold prayer? Will that make You more aware? You keep trying to embrace me.

I keep chasing things to find the next key. I am trying to force You to love me, God, but You keep saying You give that freely. How can I just sit here and be? God, I just want You to love me. But You already do.

So, help me rest while I believe that to be true. Let me stay still as You show me You're a good Dad. Help me to see You are not mad. God, I must surrender this to You, for I need a different view.

He and this story are a gift. I can't demand things; instead, I need my mind to shift. I just need hope that I hold onto every day. I want to watch Your will happen, come what may.

I know You will slow my mind. It's Your hope I need to find. Here I go, God, I surrender this to You. Help me to always remember You're the only one who can make my dreams come true.

GOD'S LOVE

"God, I want to know all about Your love. I want to know how not to look at my circumstances but live above. Right now, I am asking You what that looks like. Does that mean You will always make me do something I dislike? Do I have to feel it? Do I have to always submit? Do I get to make my own choices? Or do I have to listen to everybody else's voices? Will You kill me like You killed Paul? Will I always feel this small?

"God, I don't know what love is. The examples I have had do not act like the Bible says. I want to act in Your love and know Your love for me. But is Your love free? Do I have to work for it and be perfect? If I mess up, will Your love still have the same effect? Will Your love ever neglect?

"I have searched my whole life to find love to fill my heart. I keep thinking You don't love me, so why don't I ever want to be apart? People say I can't love them in a godly way if I don't love You. Can that be true? Because I know I love people the way You do.

"God, could that mean I already know how to love You? Is Your love a love I already knew? You tell me, *'My daughter, don't you see? Love is not a feeling, an emotion, or always setting out to agree. Love is found in us Three. It's how We always show up. It is how when you need it the most, We always fill your cup. It's how when you call on My name, I never put you to shame. I never left your side. For you, I will always provide. At your worst, I still see you as My bride.*

'Love is a choice, and I choose you. Will you choose to see Me from My point of view? My daughter, I come and pursue, for My kingdom is not complete without you. You're my princess, and I will always chase My daughter. I always want to dance with and hear her laughter. I gave him to show you what tangible love looks like. You love him even when he does things you dislike.

'My daughter, won't you choose? Will your words match your tattoos? Will I be the object of all your affections? Will you always follow My directions?

'I hope I answered all your questions. My love is not merely a suggestion. My love is what you need. Will you trust Me and let Me lead? My daughter, that is what My love is. A God who does what He says.'

"Yes, God. Go ahead and proceed. For Your love is a guarantee."

COME TO THE TABLE

"Come to the table; I have a feast just for you. I spent all this time to pursue. I want you to live like royalty. For you never have to question my loyalty. My princess and my bride, don't you see? This whole journey was to set you free.

"You are not a slave. This is not the way I want you to behave. Stop acting like you are living from a grave. You have so much worth. I made you, and I have known you since before your birth. You don't have to beg or plead. I will always provide you with what you need.

"Don't you see all this food at this table? My love for you is what makes you stable. So, stop living under a slave label. Come home to My palace. My daughter and princess, you never have to worry about your status. You are welcome here to run carefree. Your inheritance will always be a guarantee. It is what makes you a weapon. Unlike Esther, you don't have to wait to be beckoned. You are always welcome here. You never have to function in fear. I have already killed your Haman, for I am no layman. I am the King.

"Nothing stops what I sign off with my signet

ring. Your destiny is already set. Everything I set into motion can't be stopped. My plans for you cannot be swapped. My reputation is always the same. I always do what I claim.

"Come here to sit with Me at My table. See that I am more than able. Say goodbye to your enemy, for he cannot stand against you when you know your identity.

"Your victory is already won. This battle is already done. My daughter and My bride, won't you invite Me to be by your side? Tonight, your enemy will be denied. For it is you for whom I want to provide."

GOD, ARE YOU SAFE?

My whole life, I don't think I have ever felt emotionally safe. And this situation is making me feel unsafe. Do You really expect me to deal with his harassing attitude? I am trying to behave like Jesus and show him the beatitude.

However, right now, I just want to run away. God, what is it that You are trying to get me to convey? I am still trying to figure out who You are. Right now, I feel like You are just leaving a bunch of scars. I want to be who You want me to be. I really do want to be free.

Isn't there another way? For I really don't want to stay. My circumstances have not changed. Some of my most important relationships are still estranged. My home is still falling apart. But nothing is breaking more than my heart.

You keep asking me to trust You. I really am trying to, but my outlook is a hard view. The promises You are making seem to be impossible. You keep telling me I am not the one who is responsible. You will make it happen; all I do is agree. Sure, God, I will agree if I have a guarantee.

But that is not how You work. My faith waivers, and I keep going berserk. Then the question is, do I really trust You? When You're the only one that can make Your promises to me come true. What will I do when my world is falling apart? Will I still give You my heart?

When I don't feel safe in my own life, will I treat You with strife? For Your whole goal has always been my dependency on You. Your job is to make me new. Sometimes, that means trusting You through my greatest fears. It is saying I love You through all my tears.

You're the One I run to. Because through this crazy mess, You're the only thing that is true.

Are You safe, God? Well, of course not, but everything else is just a facade. My safety is not Your goal. You just want me to surrender my control, for You have great things in store for me. If only I would agree. I guess that means I surrender my safety. Making this decision did not come hastily.

I want to make You my life's priority. Therefore, I give You all authority. Here is my life, Lord. Do with it as You will. I no longer want to live life based on how I feel.

I CHOOSE TO LOVE HIM

Is this really the fairy tale You promised? I am not feeling it if I am honest.

I mean, he is kind of a mess. Of course, I can't claim to be a success. Let's face it: we both appear to be broken beyond repair. We both need countless prayers. Sometimes, I wonder what the heck You see in us. All we do is fuss. We do the wrong thing even when we have the right intentions. It seems our lives are just intervention after intervention.

It's funny how You used him to be an example of our love story. I ran and have hurt You just as much as he has, but who is keeping inventory? This fairy tale is for Your glory. I have been so consumed with who wins. I have been focused on all our sins. Like if we clean them up, would it make You work any faster? I have been obsessed with getting to the part where we need the pastor.

To be honest I have not thought of him much. Well, except to think about his touch. Do I really love him? When I think of him, I feel grim. He has not treated me very nice. I think this relationship seems to come at a very high price. Is it one I am willing to pay? Or am I just thinking about the "I do" day?

I think I am in love with the story more than him. Like if You would let us get married on a whim. Something buried in my heart says that I really do love this man. But he is the one who ran.

My need for safety keeps me from letting You or him in. This is causing a lot of feelings to stir within. God, I think You want me to make a choice. You helped me find my voice. I don't want to hide anymore. I don't want to keep fighting this war.

A decision I must make. It is time for my heart to awaken. Do I choose to love him and You even if he never pursues? Even if my fairy tale is not perfect? Even if he continues to show me very little respect? Will I choose to trust You? Even when he is not acting like You have made him new.

For this is Your story that You have written. Let's face it: it does not make me feel smitten. However, it makes me see that life is messy and painful. Sometimes, we act very shameful. I know I have more than once during this journey.

Thank goodness You're not treating me like an attorney. You choose me and say I am worthy. Even when I feel so dirty. Shouldn't I feel the same for Your son? You say he is the one. I can't keep treating him like I can throw him away. That is not the kind of love You want me to display.

I must make a choice. Will I listen to Your voice? Or will I listen to all my anxieties and fears, like I have done for twenty years? I think that game has gotten old. What if I choose to live life through a different mold? I am discovering that when I choose not to love him, I decide not to love You too.

My life has been decided from the wrong point of view. I think he is so much more than he portrays. So let my heart praise. My God gives good gifts. Let my heart shift. I choose to love You. I choose to love him, knowing one day, he will pursue. You say he is such an amazing, godly, pure, and sweet man. Well, God, I finally choose to trust in Your plan. I make no demands. I am going to leave it in Your hands.

COVERED IN GOD'S BLOOD

God, what makes me special, what makes me great? Why would You choose me to be Your date? You keep coming after me. I keep trying to flee. I was so angry again. I really have been trying to just say yes and amen. There is just one thing I still must give. One more painful memory I must relive. A story I thought was encompassed in love. It was not a love that came from above. It was a story of co-dependency and a counterfeit love. One that did not come from the true Beloved.

For all these years, I kept her wedding dress. Then I searched for the same love she had, but it always turned out to be a mess. I had a wedding day with You. You told me to cut the dress off because You want to make it new. For an entire year I looked to see if You would replace that dress. Then You picked out a dress for me, and this caused so much distress. This is not the story I dreamed of all these years. I never wanted to shed all these tears. But her love story caused my father's abuse. Look what this counterfeit love produced.

You wanted to purify all their pain and answer my parents' prayers. You wanted to show everyone how our Father cares. So, You authored this story that was so bizarre. Would this love story be the greatest ever, or just cause one big scar? No, not a scar, for I am protected by Your blood. This is what causes one big flood. Your river of life is behind the dam. This water that flows is covered by the sacrificial Lamb. It provides life and healing and refreshes the soul. It only requires that I give up control. It's the prayers from Your children that break the dam. Hammer away; give it one big slam. The time is now; it is time to bow.

Why am I special, God? Because I am covered in Your blood, which makes me a part of Your royal squad. I am a daughter of a King! This is no small thing. This is life, and it is a weapon, for I am not second. I am always on Your mind. It is the enemy You have called me to bind. When the smoke clears, my perspective changes. He is the one in chains, behind bars, guarded by angels. Trying to convince me to stay there with him. Trying to make my life seem grim. I am no prisoner; I am a princess. In God's eye, I have never been less. It's His blood that gives me authority, freedom, and a new name.

It's being covered in His blood that brings this story fame. It's His blood that gave me a new romance. Being covered in His blood taught me how to dance. I feel like a child for the first time. It's His blood that wrote all these rhymes. It's His blood that gave me a beautiful love story. It's His blood that gives Himself glory. Being covered in His blood gave me the strength to carry us through. It's His blood that is going to make Brandon new. It's His blood that makes the pain worth going through. Being covered in His blood is the only thing I live to pursue. It is His blood that is the only way I made it through. The sacrificial Lamb is the only reason I have a love story at all. It is the reason I am always in victory, and I will never fall. It is the reason I am free from suicide, alcohol, self-abuse, and a past that haunted me.

His blood is the only reason I am free. It's His blood that saves Brandon and makes him a prince. It is by His blood that I was convinced. It is by His blood that this story ends with a happily ever after. His blood is the reason I have childlike laughter. Thank You, God, for covering me in Your blood. Thank You for Your river of life coming in like a flood.

This story touches so many of Your children and covers them with love. You changed this love story to one that was written from above.

THE BRIDE

I finally found out what it means to be Your bride. To always have and hold You by my side.

I dressed up in my dress covered in white. Tonight, You want to make me the light. There is gold on my dress to show I am royalty. All I had to do was give You my loyalty. The sparkles all over my dress shimmer in Your sweet light of glory. That is why You wrote this story. Your bride I have always been. This is where my identity begins. It's a weapon to recognize who I am in Your embrace. You are always showering me with grace.

Your love is what my heart beats for. How had I never seen this before? You were fighting a big war. To die for me and claim my soul. My heart intertwined with Yours was always the goal. I am nothing without You. You have spent so much time and effort to make me new. Your promises You always keep. Your voice is what I always follow because I am Your sheep. When I think of all You have done for me, I weep.

My God, You always pursue me. Your love is the only key. My heart beats just for You. Your love is the only thing that is true. You will protect me and provide. You are my true guide. I can trust You to take care of me. As we dance our first dance, I truly feel free.

You are worth everything I have fought for. Your character and love for me is all I want to explore. I am no longer in a war. With

You by my side, I am so much more. I have always wanted a true love story. But it's not complete if it does not shine Your glory. You handed me the light so I could walk down the aisle. This walk felt like more than a mile. Along the way, I made a number of friends. Our love for You and each other was much more than we could comprehend.

You let this light of Your glory shine through the darkness. It breaks through the hearts that are full of hardness. You loved me until I finally chose to be Your bride. You look at me with so much pride. You say, *"You're beautiful and more than enough,"* even on days when I look rough. You love me even when I don't feel worthy. You walked and carried me through this entire journey. Thank You for all the love that You poured into me. For it overflowed and set me and everyone around me free.

I tried on my dress even when he said he wasn't for me. That is because I trust You enough to pick my groom. Your love that I lean on helps me bloom. It allows me to continue to see him through Your point of view. While You continue to make him new, I pray for him until he is ready to take my hand, until he is ready to agree with Your plan. I trust him because I trust You. It's Your eyes I see him through.

Because I am Your bride, I can continue to keep this hope alive. I know the prayers You give to me are the reason he thrives. It's my complete dependency on You that will keep this love growing strong. It's the reason my heart still sings your song.

My Bridegroom, You are what my heart waits upon. This victory has already been won. Our dependency on the Trinity was what this whole story depended upon.

WALK ME DOWN THE AISLE

Dad, it's time to do what you have always dreamed of since I was a little girl. I know I have always been more precious to you than pearls. I know you have mixed emotions as you give me over to him.

You know we didn't get married on a whim, for you have been praying specifically for a godly man like him. I know it is hard to give away your little girl. My eyes fill up with tears as I remember grabbing your little finger as we would twirl.

I know tears will flow down from your eyes as you watch his look when he sees me for the first time. He will see you have given him the prime. The woman he has always prayed for and dreamed of is draped on your arm.

I know you look at him and wonder, *Will he ever cause her harm?* Don't worry, Dad, because God Himself picked him out for me. It's not just you giving me away; it's the Three.

Thirty-six years ago, you had to surrender me to them. That painful decision kept me from being condemned.

As your heart is stirring and you hand me over to him, I want you to know that with a cord of three, we will always swim. There is no sinking when God is the whole plan.

I know you are wondering if he is a good man. Dad, he is kind, loving, and pure. With him, I have never been more secure.

I love you and I have always felt lucky to call you father. You are a man full of honor. So, it's time, Dad, grab my hand as we look at each other with one big smile.

Dad, it's time to walk me down the aisle.

DEATH TO SELF

Today, I mourn as I say goodbye to the old me. A death that was always a guarantee. A me that was not who I was supposed to be, for that version of me was never free. Trapped in all her fears and anxiety. She was always trying to fit into society. That is not where she belonged. In this place, she always felt like she had been wronged.

God took her through a very bizarre journey. To show her that He is not an attorney. He is not interpreting the law and presenting the facts to expose all her wrongs. He is just guiding her back to His heart, where she always belongs.

A fairy tale written just for her to enjoy. For the old her, broken, abused, and trying to hide, is who He had to destroy. That was never who He meant her to be. He had to reveal the ugly truth, for with the demons, she could no longer agree.

The flesh screamed, fought, and made a big scene. It did not want to die so she could become clean. For one year, she fought and tried to hang on. However, it was God who she needed to put her love and hope upon.

It was time for Him to take it all away. That flesh was starting to decay. It was time for something new. God continued to pursue. But to that dying flesh, it felt like a war. The flesh did not want the spirit to restore. A new life and a new hope. Learning for the first time to use God to help her cope. No more living in sin and acting out of fear. Now, she is choosing to draw near.

God is her refuge and her only source of hope. She no longer yells at Him and screams, "Nope." She dances with Him and laughs as she sits in His lap. When it comes to life, she looks to God to be her map.

Yes, the old Rachael is dead and gone. For she no longer wants to be withdrawn. She is still figuring out what she likes and who she is. She feels safe doing this if she remembers she is His. She is childlike and reborn.

There is a time to mourn. For now, she gets to explore. She must let go of the girl she was before. Don't stay there long, for this is a good thing.

Her winter has turned into spring. Say goodbye to the old me. I am in the heart of the Three.

GOD ANSWERS A FIVE-YEAR-OLD WHEN SHE CRIES

"God, I asked if You could undo what was done when I was five. This question almost caused me not to be alive. After being so vulnerable with You, I felt like You did not come through. The very next day, I grabbed my gun. I wondered, God, what have You done? Why did You bring all this up in me? Don't You see I just want to flee?

"God, after months of pain and doubt, I finally figured out what his story was all about. I tried to die to my old self. Instead, I kept holding on to fighting my own self. You kept asking me to love You, but I had to love me too.

"God, what's wrong? I really do want to be new and belong. But I keep fighting and feeling numb. Why can't I be the woman You want me to become? Why can't I love myself with the promise You give? Why am I the only one I can't forgive?

"I keep screaming for You to take him. For if you did, I swear I could finally swim. But it's not him who I felt let me sink. It was You who I thought was not in sync.

"As I try to heal and give You this last thing, it's her who keeps me from making You the King. She is mad and screaming, will

You answer my cry? She is angry, ready to fight, and she will not comply. I see You comforting her and asking her to calm down. As You hold her and tell her You will always be around.

"God, I can't keep her anymore. But she is impossible to ignore. God, will You answer and put her to rest? Will You answer her request?

> *"My daughter, I can't undo what was done when you were five. I promise you I will never deprive. My daughter, I didn't abandon you. I am the only thing that is true. I was there when you cried. I never left your side.*
>
> *"I collected every tear. I heard every prayer. Yes, I heard you when you cried. That is why I died. To give you this new life. So, you could be my wife. I don't want you to have any more fear. It has robbed you of all these years. I never abused you.*
>
> *"My daughter, I wrote this story to make you brand-new. I used those tears to water the seed that grew hope. My daughter, look through your life through My new scope.*
>
> *"You don't need her anymore. It's time to close that door. I am protecting your innocence now. If that privilege you would give me and allow. My daughter, get rid of those inner vows. It's time for you to pursue Me. My love is the only key. Let him into that place. Those scars can't cause you any more disgrace.*

"I will never leave. I just need you to believe. Come here, My daughter, accept My embrace.

"Lay your five-year-old down; let Me be what takes her place."

THE FINAL BATTLE

In the distance, I hear swords sharpening and armor clinking. I know this is all because of my thinking.

A battle is coming, and I am not prepared. This toxic thinking has left me impaired. I have never been so scared.

Angry and confused, I am still mad at You. Did I hear You wrong? I have been waiting for so long. It seems I no longer have my shoes. Not since you brought me the bad news. Those shoes of peace I took off hours ago. Now, I am back in a dark place I never thought I would go. Are You still the God I know?

I stood in faith and went against my old ways. I did not account for all these delays. Now, I am standing here, and I lead my troops. But the battle isn't here; what am I supposed to tell them, "Oops"?

I feel like a fool, and I feel crazy. I know this isn't because I was lazy. I prayed, laid down fleeces, and asked for godly advice. This letdown seems to come at too high of a price.

The enemy did not waste any time. He got his troops ready and tried to commit a crime.

God, this battle is getting too tough. I feel like I am alone and I am not enough. The liar is speaking, and I am beginning to agree. The things he says are the only things I see. I can't go back to Egypt to be a slave. Trying to go back there will only take me to my grave. This wilderness is getting rough. You yell at me, "My daughter, that is enough."

I close my eyes, and I see I am not alone. There are angels fighting all around me, and You are sitting on Your throne. The angel looks at me; I can see he is fighting hard. He says, "You must believe." This was not said with a gentle regard. "We will lose if you keep fighting for the enemy. You must stop agreeing with him and find your identity. The promised land is up ahead. You keep choosing the wilderness instead."

I opened my eyes, and I decided to fight. I realized I must be the light. This battle was not easy, and it was not right.

God, how could I keep forgetting who You are? Every time I do, I begin acting so bizarre. I can't keep doing this anymore. I no longer want to be a part of this war. God, You don't change, but I must. You must be the only thing that I trust. I choose to face the giants in the promised land. I choose to do it while holding Your hand.

As I look back, I see the enemy. It seems he is in chains, for that is his identity. He never could lay a hand on me.

I will let You win this battle and choose to be free. It is time I made my decree. I am the bride of Christ!

THE WEDDING FEAST

As Your bride, I wait for You. I see that You are the only thing that is true.

I have my lamp ready to light the way. I brought enough oil in case You don't come today. I won't give up. I will be a bride waiting. I await with excitement as my imagination is busy creating.

I see You laughing and dancing in my mind. Your smile is so kind. All the brides laugh and talk about all Your promises. We jest about how we won't be doubting Thomases.

Wait, what is that we hear? Is that You coming for us, my dear?

Some realize they no longer have the light. I guess they were not expecting You tonight. I had brought enough oil, but it came at a high price. I didn't even think twice, for You are my King, my Bridegroom, and my Redeemer. You had to restore me back to being a dreamer. I see You are attracted to the light. Your laughter, love, and glory break through the night.

You lovingly approach me. You tell me it's time to be free. You see me in all my glory. You say I have no spot or wrinkle but am blameless and holy.

You see, I have made myself ready. In Your love, I remain steady. I hear you say, *"It's time, My bride, for Me to take you to the wedding feast I have prepared for you."*

We ride off together, for we are way overdue. I hear the other brides calling, but You say, *"I do not know you."* The wedding feast door was shut to them. Their inability to be made ready caused them to be condemned.

I hear You whisper, *"I am righteously jealous for you."* Therefore, You will always pursue.

I no longer want to have idols. For You're the only one I want to walk with down the aisle.

I am clothed in fine linen, bright and pure. For You are my Husband, the Lord of Hosts, the Holy One of Israel, Redeemer, God of the whole earth, so I am secure.

I hear in the distance an angel saying, "Blessed are those who are invited to the marriage supper of the Lamb." I can hardly contain myself as I realize that is who I am.

My identity is the bride of Christ. I was bought at a very high price. Make yourself ready, all you brides, for you do not want to miss all that the Lord provides.

AM I TOO MUCH?

God, I have been wondering; I have a few questions to ask. Are my problems too much to unmask?

I have been hiding all these years. I have hidden all my tears. In my trouble, I tried to let people in. That's when my life started to spin. Is my suicidal tendency too much of a sin?

The church seems to be prepared for all kinds of traumas and addictions. But no one seems to be able to deal with my affliction.

Is this pain too much for Your grace? Am I too hard to embrace? Will anyone be able to run this race?

I have struggled with this all these years. I have dealt with my fears. But one still remains. Is this affliction always going to keep me in chains?

I just want someone to hold my hand. I just want someone to understand. I am not trying to hurt anyone. For this is a battle You already have won.

Why does everyone keep throwing this in my face? Why won't they just help me run this race? I have been hurt by groups that were meant to keep me protected. Unfortunately, I had to leave because it was infected.

I was taken out of my position. I was given no recognition. All people saw was my issue of trying not to hurt myself. Maybe they are trying to protect themselves.

I just wish someone would stay. I want to be myself and for people not to walk away. I wish they would sit with me in this mess. That is how this journey will become a success. I wish my miracle wasn't so hard to believe. Sometimes, I just want to leave.

However, that is not an option. This is part of my adoption. I can't be Your daughter or bride with all these lies inside.

There were parts of me that died. I just wish I had more friends, family, and my church by my side.

When I see Your body on that cross, Your answer is coming across. My suicidal tendencies and my miracles are not too much for You. You did all this to make me new. Your bloodstained body gave me the answers that I needed. You have already succeeded.

Let me reveal this fairy tale about a King who came after His princess. She will no longer live like a slave, for in His eyes, she has never been less. She is the daughter He died for and for who He went through all-out war.

No, I am not too much for the King. He took me back to the castle where the sound of my freedom and love for Him would always sing.

CAN YOU STOP HER?

"She is angry, filled with rage. She is definitely not acting her age.

"She is kicking, screaming, shouting, and fighting. There is nothing about her that is inviting.

"She hits me and hurts me without a care. God, she is not acting very fair.

"She calls me names and tells me she hates me. She is trying to get me to agree.

"Her hate is like insanity. The way she speaks to me is the worst kind of profanity.

"She is the source of all my tears. She is the reason for all my fears.

"No one has treated me with more abuse. She still tries to seduce.

"Her words are lies, but I find them so easy to believe. Why don't I just ask her to leave?

"She keeps beating me into submission. I hate her yet keep giving her permission.

"She is ruining my life. She always treats me with strife.

"No one has tormented me like her. I want to hide from her, but where?

"Her safety net is like a jail. Her protection is like a noose around my neck, and I am getting pale.

"God, don't You see, can't You stop her?"

"My daughter, I am right here. Why did it take you a year?

"Don't you see I have always been bigger than that abusive girl? I have always offered you My pearls.

"Why do you throw them away? No, I do not delay.

"I can see that you are being abused. I know that you feel confused. Yes, daughter, I see you are bruised.

"My daughter, I offer you My unending joy. This is not about a boy.

"It's about this abusive girl. You're My daughter with whom I want to dance and twirl.

"If you want to stop her, you must choose. You must stop the abuse.

"My daughter, I have tried to stop this madness. I want to end this sadness.

"My daughter, will you walk away? This girl is you; will you stop her abuse today?"

GOD GAVE ME A VOICE

Sometimes, I feel like I really messed up this year. It turns out that things are not always as they appear. God's direction is not always very clear.

There are valleys, mountains, dips, turns, and even doors. We will make it through as long as God's love is what our heart yearns for.

Somewhere along this crazy journey, my insecurities got a hold of me, and I lost focus. That, of course, is how Satan gets in and provokes us.

My whole life, I have heard God loud and clear. Unfortunately, I never learned how to draw near. I was drowning in all my doubts, insecurities, and fears. So, I made a vow that I would not shed tears.

For no one answers when you cry. Well, that is the lie I was willing to believe until I died.

However, God came in and tore my universe apart. I thought He broke my heart.

I have always had a strong voice. I just did not use it by choice.

I used it as a safety net. I protected myself when I thought You were a threat. Then I would quickly throw You away and forget. I did not want to be upset.

I did not realize how hard my heart became until I started to play love like a game. I always felt shame.

A childhood lost. Abuse that came at an excessive cost.

A failure is how I always felt. I thought this was the hand with which I was dealt.

So, I became so strong in myself that no one even questioned if I was losing my sanity. I had too much pride and vanity.

God told me I had to be different. I thought my fairy tale would be magnificent.

I tried to make God's plan come true, which cost me my voice. I felt like I no longer had a choice.

I blamed Him and His plan for taking the abuse. I used to identify as a victim as an excuse.

Till finally, I had taken too much. I have always feared people's touch.

That is why when I started to drown, I didn't want anyone around. So, I drowned.

I didn't want to take Your hand. But God, this was always Your plan.

You came and saved me and sent a whole army. Your plan was never to harm me.

You just wanted me to draw near. To make Your love for me truly clear.

I had to lean on You completely.

You started to whisper to me sweetly, *"My daughter, if you're dependent on Me, then I will show you how to be free. I gave you a strong voice, but you must be humble. It's love that is missing; that is why you always stumble. I never meant for you to be strong on your own. Your strength and powerful voice come from Me being on My throne."*

When I realized this, my insecurity and anxiety faded. I no longer needed to be persuaded.

God speaks to me clearly. I must take His voice sincerely.

No more looking at my circumstances or situations. No more getting mad about complications.

God gave me a voice to show I am not a victim. God adopted me, therefore I have beat the system.

God loves me dearly, and I am full of His wisdom and discernment. I don't need the world's opinions and reimbursement.

Satan, you can no longer steal my identity. God's voice in me brings serenity.

He has put me in situations to stand up and kick out the enemy. I now realize that Satan and doing things in my own power had become my frenemy.

I see you and what you are because God has kicked you out. I do not need to shout.

God's truth is a weapon. It slaughters depression. I am not silenced by you anymore. God already won the war.

I will speak with truth, love, and humility. For this is my identity. This is God's answer for how I stop the abuse and live in serenity.

I finally realized I have a choice. God gave me back my real voice.

CINDERELLA

When I started this journey, someone prophesied that I had a fairy tale with God. They said it was *Cinderella* because I was acting like a slave and living a facade.

My Father's inheritance said that was not true. I just need to change my point of view. Cinderella was never a slave. It was the harsh abuse she suffered from her stepmother and sisters that caused her to cave. So, a slave is how she behaved. Just because her circumstances look a certain way does not mean things are how they are portrayed.

I have been acting like a slave my whole life. That is why I wasn't ready to be his wife. God said, "This is enough. This life was never supposed to be this rough." He came running after me. I finally saw that He paid for my inheritance and made me free. I did not want to agree.

My mind has been a mess for all these years. I have caused my own tears. Letting my stepmom and sisters decide how I lived. It is amazing that I survived. For they are not family; they are the enemy. Living in my own filth and forgetting my identity. "Cinderella, do this and do that." My life became flat. I created a fantasy world to escape the pain. Disgusting thoughts that ran around in my brain. All to support a facade of control. All I was doing was hurting my soul.

What is the big deal? I am not hurting anyone. I am not acting it out, but somehow, Satan is acting like he already won. For if he can capture your mind. Then, he will always keep you blind.

How could I love when I was turning it to be so disgusting? In my mind, I was lusting. I was stuck in a life that was settling for slavery. The whole while, I thought I was acting bravely. Taking on their chores and demands. When I was the authority, they should have been taking my commands. I did not know what love was; I did not know how to take Your hand. In my filth and rags, I stayed. Acting like I was a maid.

> God said, "You are royalty. I just need you to capture your thoughts and give Me your loyalty. My love for you has paved the way. I just need you to stay. You keep running back to that place. You are running a hard race. I am trying to extend My grace. Please, won't you choose Me to embrace? It is My character upon which you must stand. You are the one on whom I will pour all My love like a firebrand. Stop running back to all your abuse. Just look at what it has produced. It cannot take away your pain. Lust does not satisfy; it only creates a chain. It keeps you from creating good boundaries and from doing the right thing. It never satisfies; it only makes your mood swing. It gives you temporary pleasure but ends in permanent guilt. This was not the way that love was built. Here I am to save you once again. If you do not trust Me now, then when? Yes, I sent a prince. That was never meant to convince. That is why I took him away for a little while. No, this

isn't a trial. My daughter, you never needed him to be the princess. I already paid the price, and you have never been less. I needed you to see who I really am. I am the sacrificial Lamb. I am your fairy tale. I died for you to take away the abuse, lust, and facade you called love create a merry tale. It's about a Father and a King. You, as His daughter, already had His inheritance paid for. Don't you see, My daughter, love is what I wanted to restore. You are not a slave; you're a princess I will always pursue. This is the only identity that is true. The prince is not how you become royalty. He is the gift that I give you joyfully. I am your true fairy tale; won't you live happily ever after with Me?"

BEAUTY AND THE BEAST

A tale made in God's design. A song He has written that is divine. Hearts that never change. Relationships that are estranged.

Neither one is willing to break. Each one blaming each other for their own mistakes. Pride that is suffocating. Apologies were awaiting.

What a broken mess we have become. Wounds that make us numb. We are one decision away from being a beast. A beauty we are waiting to be released.

A Savior we need. If only we would wait on Him to proceed. For God is waiting on us to ask Him to lead. We are too busy trying to protect ourselves. No one is willing to be vulnerable and expose themselves. Too scared to admit we need each other. Too much pain and pride to stick closer to than a brother. Stuck in our own ways. Acting like we are a bunch of strays. Forgetting we were bought at a deadly cost. Still holding onto sins that were washed.

A beast we all have been. Needing beauty to change us within. For that to happen, we would need to invite them into the mess. Our deepest dreams and needs, we must express.

Look, we are beginning to change. Going against emotions that feel so strange. One of us had to pursue. So, we both could be made new.

God came after me. His love was my missing key. Now, I can offer you unconditional love, too. Changing you from a beast to his beauty so you can also pursue. Hearts that quickly change are motives and priorities rearranged.

This is the original love story that He gave to me. The only way we both would become free.

It's been twelve years in the making. It took a great amount of praying and shaking. We were both the beauty and the beast in this fairy tale. In the end, God made it the perfect love story and such a merry tale.

He planned our whole story and wedding around this poem and His glory. What an amazing, godly love story. He took His two broken children and restored them, for He did not want either of them to feel condemned. Both came with a deep scar. Neither of them realized how God's healing would take them so far.

Beauty and the Beast.

DOORS WE MUST GO THROUGH

During this journey, I went through lots of doors. Behind each door was a series of wars.

Memories that haunted me. Things I hide down deep so I could never be free.

Jesus has taken my hand and walked me through. So He could undo the lies and show me what was true.

I went kicking and screaming. He just keeps on redeeming.

He waits for me as I count my costs and make tough decisions. He keeps giving me such beautiful visions.

A dreamer He wanted me to be. But death is the only thing I could see.

That is why each door has been so painful. God continues to be so faithful.

A choice He says I must make. I keep saying, "No, God, let's take a break."

I want to put all of this on the back burner. God knows I am not a slow learner.

He tells me I am not a slave, that I need to stop living like I have one foot in the grave.

"My daughter, you have always had a choice. It's important to Me that you know you have a voice. Stop choosing Me and then yelling I am making you do it as an excuse! Look at all this anger that this has produced. If you choose to do what I ask, that is no small task. But you can't blame Me every time he hurts you. Saying to Me, 'Look at what You are putting me through.' You must choose to follow My plan. Then trust Me to give you the right man. Do you really think you can do better? My daughter, you forgot your place; you are a debtor. I paid your price, so stop fighting Me. I need you to choose life and start living like you are free. You don't trust Me, and you don't trust him. You keep asking Me to swim. How can you swim when you keep choosing to drown? You keep trying to hide and choose for no one to be around. I am meeting you tonight. It is time you join the right fight."

God woke me up and told me to pray. I tried to go back to sleep and say not today.

I asked, "Whom am I praying for?"

"You, my daughter, it's time to open the last door."

Jesus came to hold my hand. He said, *"You are going to need Me for this; soon, you will understand."*

I started walking, but my heart felt heavy. Is it really time to do this already?

Jesus said, *"You told me that you would choose life. Yet you are still living and constantly choosing to feel strife.*

"Let us go back to that dark place. Don't worry; I will show you grace."

My heart started to pound, and tears started to come down. There I was at twelve, thirteen, fourteen, and on with the biggest frown.

Obsessed with death and tormented. Just praying to God and hoping the storm would end.

I didn't just lose my childhood; I lost my whole life being addicted to death. This realization took my breath.

I could not stop crying as I realized how tormented I have always been. A new life I must want to begin.

Jesus was crying, too. For this is not the life He wanted me to view.

"This is what your addiction to death has done. My daughter, do you want to have fun? Open that door that says life. It must be your choice to become My wife. You are not a slave. My daughter, please be brave. Open the door and walk through. I want to make you brand new."

I opened the door and chose to live life and leave death behind. A million thoughts were going through my mind.

Is it safe, and *will I enjoy the new world I am about to walk into?* As I opened that door, I saw a whole new view.

There was sunshine, clouds, dips, mountains, hills, and valleys. Jesus says, *"Don't worry, I am by your side; there will be bad times, but you will always rally. Life is hard, but it is worth living.*

My love is always forgiving. So come on, My daughter, it is time to walk through life together. We can make it through any weather."

LOVE AT A HIGH PRICE

"As I lay broken on the floor, I beg You, God, please no more. I am weary and tired. How much more of my soul do You require? I know You did not spare any of Yours. My tears and my prayers, You will not ignore. I know You hear me, God, I know You care. So, why does my human heart still believe You are not fair?

"It is not faith that I lack. It is Your motives that I attack. Why are You honoring them? For they are the ones You should condemn. Why are You not answering me? Haven't I been the one who has been preaching about Your love that helps people become free? Did You forget about me? Don't You see that I am weary. Haven't I been preaching about Your theory? Knowledge, I have, but one thing I lack: it is Your unending love that I want back.

"The condemned accepted You so freely, for they did not hold any expectations. Here, I am counting all my limitations. Acting like I am exempt. Holding You in contempt. Forgetting that I was in chains. Just remembering all my pain. How could I forget Yours? You sent Your son down to pay for our sins, which caused pain He had to endure. He cried tears of blood but still shed His. Here, we are still doubting what He says.

"Love that came at the ultimate price. He didn't even think twice. His body hung on a cross as the Father cried for such loss. Here we still sit, trying to be our own boss. Thinking we know better. Forgetting we are debtors. Asking, 'Do You hear me?' The whole time, You are walking across the sea, asking me to step out in faith and draw near. As I step out, my doubts still make me feel unclear. My circumstances still cause me fear.

"You catch me and say, *'Peace be still.'* Your hand grabs for me, and You hold me close as my hope refills. Jesus, never let me go. For without You and Your love, what do I know? I would be lost except for Your love that came at a high cost.

"You may let me get lost at sea, so You can come rescue me to let me see. I am nothing without You. I am completely dependent on You to make me new. If You let me grow hungry, it is so You can feed me. You do this to set me free. A doubter, angry, prideful, and unyielding was my old way. After placing my life, faith, and love in You, I will never be the same.

"I know I am always on Your mind. Your love is patient and kind. It does not envy; it is not boastful, arrogant, or rude. It does not seek its own way, put us to shame and should not be ruled by our mood. Your love rejoices in truth as it brings hope, endures, and never ends. God, will You sit with me in my mess, for I know we are more than friends. I need Your love to come save me. I want You to set me completely free. Why would You choose to love me and pay such an excessive cost?"

> *"My daughter, I chose you because you are worthy. I enjoyed your entire journey. You are special, and you are strong. We love to dance with you, so you know you belong. You push through your pain to bring others joy. The enemy you seek out to destroy. You stand up for the broken and hurting. You let Us shine through you, so Our love is converting. Your bravery in sharing*

this story will change so many people's lives. We love the way your heart always gives. My daughter, We see you, and We love you. Our love that came at a high price was meant to pursue. That is why We will always choose you."

THE WILDERNESS

At first, I did not want to go on this journey. I always thought it would end on a gurney. I never thought I could make it through. I never expected to see life through this new view. I was just hoping to survive. I never actually thought that I would thrive.

God had me walk through the wilderness. I never have been more of a mess. I was kicking, screaming, and threatening to end my life. I have never treated God with more strife. Yelling at Him for not being fair. Acting like He didn't care. The whole time, He walked with me and never left my side. He humbled me and continued to break my pride. It was in my weakness that He made me strong. This is how it was supposed to be all along. I became so dependent on Him. Instead of fear, I started worshiping and singing hymns.

I started inviting Him for tea. This is when I started to get set free. I would walk with Him after sinning and feeling at my worst. He always meets me, and our conversations covered me in His love that immersed, for pain is the reality that I always lived in. I loved encounters with Him, but then I would start to spin. Leaving my reality of pain was a hard thing to do. He always pursued. I started to dance with Him, laugh, and twirl. He would say, "You are My favorite girl."

Still, the wilderness is hard to walk through. But it is the place where God made me new. Before the wait in the wilderness, I really did not know You. Now I am dependent on You and know Your love and goodness are true. You had to carry me because I was so weak. It made me rely on You, and now You're the only approval I seek. You have been so near to me, for You are attracted to my broken heart. I never want to feel apart.

I never took the time to dance, drink tea, or invite You to dinner until this season. Now I am looking for any reason. To spend time with You is my favorite thing to do. When I am afraid and feel anxious, my secret place is with You. I close my eyes, and I meet You under a tree, or at the campfire, or lie with You in the boat during a storm. My secret place with You is where You transform.

I had to be stuck and held in place, for this made me change from looking at Your blessings to seeking Your face. When I see Your face, I see Your smile as You laugh with me. I see Your tears when things happen to me that make me want to flee. Your hand is always reaching out. You never shout. Your gentleness and grace are all I see. Your look of compassion sets me free.

I decided to wash Your feet. I confessed my sins to You, but I did not want to retreat. I cried as I embraced You and let You wipe away my tears. I crawled into Your lap as You took all my fears. I could not let go of You, for I wanted You to renew. I left the old me and let her die. It's time to say goodbye.

I got up and danced with You. I had the best time as You made me new. But it's time to leave the wilderness behind. For it is the promised land I have in mind. I grab Your hand and say, "Let's go." For Your presence is the only promised land I want to know. Let's face the giants hand in hand. I am looking forward to the flow of milk and honey in this land.

If you see me drinking tea, dancing, or eating dinner alone and laughing without a care, know it's me in the promised land with God, for He answered my prayer!

FINDING HOME

What a journey I have been on. When I started drafting my first blog and this book over a year ago, I never thought it would take this long to complete the story. In fact, the story is not finished. At first, I did not understand why God put me through so much. Then, I realized that God did not put me through anything. I did this to myself when I refused to adhere to the guidelines that He gave me.

I discovered that I did not love myself or act like His daughter and bride. My defense was to control my environment and manipulate God, thinking I could convince Him to give me His grace and love. When that did not work, I tried to hurt myself so He would show me sympathy. God showed me grace anyway, but my manipulative and controlling ways were not what caused Him to love me. It was in my humility, brokenness, and complete surrender that I saw who God is in me and my identity in Him.

I was a mess and had seemingly lost everything. I realized that doing things my way only resulted in torment. I recognized that the only good thing in me is God. So, finally, I let go. I started cooperating with what God was doing in me. I saw that I had been letting everyone else's behavior affect my identity and purpose. I was living like a victim instead of a victor. I acted like I was strong, but I was scared and dying from my own insecurities. Then I realized I could not hide or pretend anymore. I had to be accountable. I had to surrender all control. This was the beginning of my healing.

It cost me my life to surrender all control. The old Rachael died, and the Rachael God had created was born. Through the pain, heartache, disappointment, false hope, and broken dreams, the real me appeared. Losing everything and being humbled showed me that standing on the firm foundation of God was a better way. I am learning to be completely dependent on Him. I've realized that my circumstances are always changing, but God is always the same. The only way to gain hope, joy, and peace is to rely on God and His true character. I could finally see that my image of who I think God should be was not the truth. He is not the small-minded abuser I thought He was, and He won't be manipulated by me. It was in my surrender to the Living God that I met my heavenly Daddy and Bridegroom.

This book is a tale of a King who saved His daughter, who was suffering as she continued to live with abuse, trauma, pain, control, and manipulation. It is a tale of a King who saw a princess who thought she was a slave. He walked her through the only story that would work for her so that she would embrace freedom, love, and happiness. It is her story about finding out who the King really is, but more importantly, who she is.

Knowing that I am royalty, experiencing His unconditional love, and realizing that His gentle and kind friendship is real freedom.

And she lived happily ever after!

"But you are a chosen people, a royal priesthood, a holy nation, a people for God's own possession, to proclaim the virtues of Him who called you out of darkness into His marvelous light" (1 Peter 2:9).

Printed in the USA
CPSIA information can be obtained
at www.ICGtesting.com
CBHW051044081124
17085CB00006B/9